MAR 0 7 2017

A Truck Full of Money

RANDOM HOUSE
NEW YORK

A
TRUCK
FULL OF
MONEY

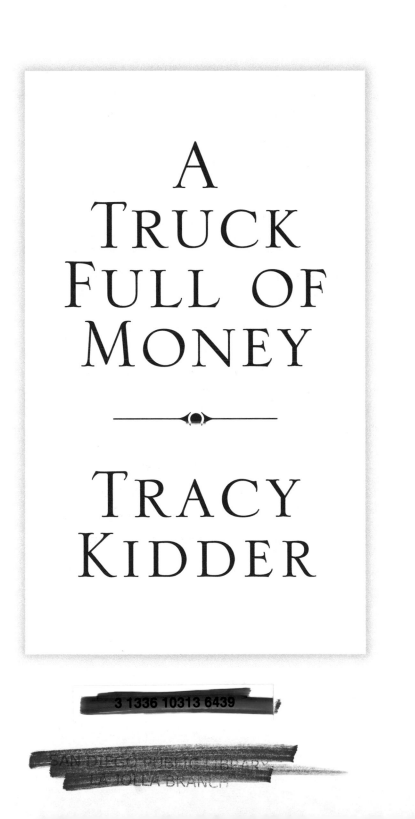

TRACY
KIDDER

Published in the United States by Random House, an imprint and division of
Penguin Random House LLC, New York.

RANDOM HOUSE and the HOUSE colophon are registered trademarks of
Penguin Random House LLC.

Library of Congress Cataloging-in-Publication Data

Names: Kidder, Tracy, author.

Title: A truck full of money / Tracy Kidder.

Description: First edition. | New York : Random House, [2016]

Identifiers: LCCN 2015050454 | ISBN 9780812995244 (hardback) |
ISBN 9780812995251 (ebook)

Subjects: LCSH: English, Paul M., 1963– | Businesspeople—United States—
Biography. | Internet industry—United States. | Information technology—United
States. | Venture capital—United States. | Entrepreneurship—United States. |
Wealth—United States. | BISAC: BIOGRAPHY & AUTOBIOGRAPHY /
Science & Technology. | BUSINESS & ECONOMICS / E-Commerce / General
(see also COMPUTERS / Electronic Commerce). | BIOGRAPHY &
AUTOBIOGRAPHY / General.

Classification: LCC HC102.5.E55 K53 2016 | DDC 338.7/610250691—dc23
LC record available at lccn.loc.gov/2015050454

International edition ISBN 978-0-399-58955-3

Printed in the United States of America on acid-free paper

randomhousebooks.com

2 4 6 8 9 7 5 3 1

First Edition

Book design by Susan Turner

For Jandi Kidder and Gene Bukhman

Choose any American at random, and he should be a man of burning desires, enterprising, adventurous, and, above all, an innovator.

—ALEXIS DE TOCQUEVILLE, *Democracy in America*

AUTHOR'S NOTE

IN THE EARLY 1980S I WROTE A BOOK ABOUT A TEAM OF ENGINEERS who were building a new computer's hardware. About thirty years later, I thought it would be interesting to look into the world of computing, and in particular the craft and business of making software. I knew Paul English only in his role as a philanthropist. I had never heard him speak about his day job, but I knew it had to do with software and that he was successful at it. So I asked him to show me around. After a while I began to feel that my guide should become my subject. What I actually said was: "Why don't I write about *you?*"

It was some time—months, I think—before he answered. I remember the moment well. He agreed, with a proviso that I had never heard before in my years as a reporter and writer.

"You have to promise not to make me look better than I am," he said.

A Truck Full of Money

PASSWORD

THE MAN ON THE STAGE IN THE JACKET AND TIE, THE HEADMASTER, invited the new seventh graders to look at the names that graced the walls around them. Paul and his classmates, 350 boys and girls, turned their faces upward. A band of surnames, painted in large black letters, ran along the summits of the auditorium's impossibly high walls. These, the headmaster said, were great Americans who had come before them here, at the oldest public school in America, Boston Latin.

Paul recognized some of the names on the frieze. Franklin, that would be Benjamin, and John Hancock and Samuel Adams and Joseph Kennedy. Knowing those names was just part of growing up in Boston. Paul loved music and played the piano and was learning the trumpet, and he knew that Bernstein must be Leonard. Some of the others sounded familiar, such as Emerson, and Paul gathered that all the rest were part of history, too: Santayana, Mather, Sumner, Brooks, and twenty more. And, said the headmaster, the new students should take note: One space had been left open up there in that pantheon. Maybe one of *them* would fill it someday.

Paul was impressed, but as he gazed up, he noticed the lightbulbs in the distant ceiling and his eyes and thoughts were drawn to them. It wasn't the kind of thing he talked about with his friends, but he always felt taken away by light and the play of light on surfaces. He could get through an entire boring sermon at St. Theresa's by studying the hanging lamps and the shadows they threw. For a while he gazed up, thinking how hard it must be to replace those lightbulbs.

The voice from the podium called him back. Over the next six years, one in three of them would flunk out, the headmaster said. They might be the top seventh graders in Boston, but this was a school where even the best had to work hard. And that meant homework, four to six hours of homework a night, said the headmaster.

Paul stared at the man. In his mind, he spoke to him. *Fuck you. I will never do homework.*

There were things he would do, though, because he wanted to do them. He tried out for the school band and made the cut, and he also decided to check out the Computer Club. It had a faculty adviser and, for a clubhouse, a windowless room down in the basement, equipped with six terminals. They looked like TVs. But they had keyboards in front of them, which meant you could tell these TVs what to do, and that made all the difference. Paul had never liked TV. He called it "the stupid box." He would watch his father watching the evening news after a day at Boston Gas. His father would sit in his easy chair with his box of Cheez-Its and his Manhattan, looking at pictures of car crashes and murder victims. And Paul would wonder to himself why his dad would want to just sit and look at what somebody else wanted him to see, and listen to strangers tell him what he should buy.

This past summer, at the Dedham Mall, Paul had discovered

something much better than television, an arcade game called Pong. The machine looked like a TV but you could control what happened on its screen. You turned a knob and these vertical lines—they worked like paddles—moved up and down on the sides of the screen, intercepting the ball that moved across the screen. A computer was even more interesting, once he began to learn how to make use of one. This didn't take long. The faculty adviser seemed like a smart guy, and it was easy for Paul to listen carefully to him, because he had information Paul wanted.

Boston Latin possessed only one actual computer, called an IBM System/34. It was locked away in a room somewhere in the basement. A student couldn't get near it. But you could communicate with it via the terminals in the Computer Club lab—"dumb terminals," because they were merely conduits between you and the actual machine. You sat down and turned on one of the terminals—they were ranged along the concrete-block walls—and the screen came alive with this message, written in green letters against a black background:

```
Please enter username _____
Please enter password _____
```

You used keys on the keyboard to move the cursor to the right spot on the screen. You typed in the letters of your username and password, and up came a menu of things that you could tell the computer to do. It was like magic the first time this happened, like a picture appearing on the surface of the blank piece of paper that came out of his father's Polaroid camera. But this happened faster, and when the menu appeared, it was just a beginning. You could *program* a computer to do any number of things.

The instructor showed Paul and the other students how to begin to exercise this power. This computer's customary language was called FORTRAN IV. Within a couple of sessions with the instructor, Paul knew the basics.

In grade school, one of his friends had given him the nickname Speed. He chose Speed for his username in the computer room. Messing around down there was already much more fun than anything in any of his classes. And then one day early in the fall term he happened to be standing behind the computer teacher, and he saw the teacher's menu appear on the terminal's screen. Paul couldn't make out the words on the list, but he could see that the teacher's menu was much, much longer than the one that came up when a student logged in.

Paul's thoughts came fast and in a package. *He has more commands than me, I need those commands, how do I get those commands?*

The ride home from school required two MBTA buses, the first to Forest Hills in Jamaica Plain and the second to West Roxbury, out on the southwestern border of Boston. It is a part of the city that didn't feel like the city to Paul, especially not on his walk home from the bus stop. His street, Perham Street—"Per-ham" was how everyone said it—had asphalt sidewalks lined with maple trees and mostly small, wood-framed, two-story houses with gabled roofs and tidy patches of grass and front porches two or three lawn chairs wide. In these days of early fall, when the maples were on the verge of turning into flowers, the street after school was filled with kids and with joyful-sounding yells—games of street hockey, dodgeball, kick the can breaking out every few hundred feet. Paul loved walking down his street then, as if through a huge birthday party, full of different entertainments, which went on and on until the voices of mothers and older sisters began calling from the front porches, calling kids home to dinner.

According to a story Paul had seen in *The Boston Globe*, the city's most populous intersection was only a block away. All four houses on that corner contained eight kids or more. But he knew a lot of other houses just as crowded. There were seven kids in his. It was a small house, considering—one bathroom and three bedrooms for nine people. Paul and his next-older brother, Danny, slept in the attic. The house felt even smaller when his parents weren't getting along. They didn't yell or hit each other, but their silences were almost worse. And one of his brothers seemed always to be getting in trouble, and another seemed dark and brooding and unhappy. Paul was the sixth of the seven. His parents had told him it was his job to take care of his little sister. As his brother Danny would say, Paul beat the *fuck* out of the last kid who had picked on her. Paul was skinny but tall for his age, and lately he'd been getting into a lot of fights. Some were bruising draws, but he hadn't lost one yet, and he always thought he would win because he was always angrier than the other kid. At home, however, he would look around the house and wonder, "Who's angry today?" It was also his job to keep the peace. Not that anyone ever told him this. It just felt like his job.

Mornings were hurried. His turn in the bathroom was fifteen minutes, starting at a quarter to six. Then it was out on his bike to deliver *The Boston Globe*, then onto the buses for school. Several thousand of the city's twelve-year-olds had taken the admission test for Boston Latin last spring. Paul had scored eighth highest and felt surprised and irritated that seven others had done better. He had always been a quick study. It took him a night's sleep and a morning's thought on the buses to come up with a plan for stealing the computer teacher's password.

His solution was like a little true story that hadn't happened yet. It went like this: The teacher sits down at a terminal in the Computer Club lab and doesn't realize that a program has been loaded into it—Paul's program, which produces on the screen not the real log-in but a nearly perfect fake. The unsuspecting teacher types his username and password into the fake log-in. Then he presses the Enter key, and Paul's program tells the computer to send those lines of text to the printer, which prints out the teacher's username and password. Paul retrieves that printout. Meanwhile, his program has already started covering its tracks. While the printer is still clacking across the room, Paul's program tells the computer to send an error message to the teacher's terminal. The teacher sees these words flash up on his screen: INCORRECT PASSWORD. PLEASE ENTER AGAIN. Finally, Paul's program deletes itself from the central computer's memory. Whereupon, automatically, the legitimate program takes over, the instructor's screen goes black, and the real log-in message appears. All of this happens fast, and the teacher, in Paul's story, doesn't think anything untoward has happened. He assumes he made a mistake typing his password. He logs in again and goes about his business.

It took Paul a few after-school sessions in the clubhouse to create the actual program. The job was complicated by the fact that when you turned off one of the terminals, everything you'd created on it disappeared for good. To save your work, you had to tell the terminal to instruct the computer to send your program to the punch-card machine—it converted your code into patterns of holes cut into stiff pieces of paper about the size of business envelopes. When you wanted to reenter your work into a terminal, you slid your punch cards, one after another, into a slot in the machine. Paul had finished an entire version of his program and saved it on punch cards when it occurred to him that he shouldn't assume the teacher wouldn't be suspicious. The printer was a noisy dot matrix. What if the teacher heard it start running and went over to find out what was being printed, and saw his own username and password appear?

Paul revised his program so that the computer would encrypt

the teacher's information before sending it to the printer. If, for example, the instructor's password was ACORN123, the program would add three letters to the letters and three numbers to the numbers, and if the teacher looked at the printout, he'd just see gibberish: DFRUQ456.

Paul sent his revised program to the punch-card machine and received thirty cards, which he numbered because they would have to be inserted into a terminal in the correct order.

There was one further complication. He had studied the teacher's habits. The man came to the lab in the morning before the first bell and logged in and did some work, but he didn't always use the same terminal. So Paul would have to load his program into each of the six terminals. He did this on a morning in late September. He got to the computer lab very early, with his punch cards concealed in his bookbag, and he went from terminal to terminal, inserting the cards one after the other and in the proper order. He finished loading all six terminals while the lab was still empty.

Everything went according to his plan. The instructor arrived a while later, logged in, saw the error message, and evidently thought nothing of it. He simply logged in again and didn't seem to notice the printer's brief clacking, or Paul's walking nonchalantly to the machine and tearing off the tongue of paper it had just produced. Later, in class, Paul took the paper out of his trousers pocket and decoded the teacher's username and password.

He took his stolen secrets to the lab right after school. A few other boys were still there when he entered. Their presence made the dismal room feel dangerous. He liked that feeling, like a color change inside him. Paul had been practicing at nonchalance forever, making himself look confident when, as usual, he was feeling shy, and calm when, as at this moment, every sight and sound was amplified. In this, his father was his model, a master of studied nonchalance. Paul and his brothers and sisters liked to say that if their father was telling a story at the dining room table and a bomb went off across the street and they turned to look, the old man would be disappointed with them, even insulted—they thought a bomb was more interesting than his story?

Paul sauntered into the Computer Club lab. He glanced at the other kids staring at their terminals. He didn't hurry. He picked an unoccupied terminal, entered the teacher's username and password, and then at last the teacher's special menu rose up on the screen. Paul had to clamp his lips shut. *Holy shit!* There were at least a dozen special commands and new places to go. Paul opened each. The most interesting was labeled ATTENDANCE. Somebody, probably the computer teacher himself, had created an electronic system for recording attendance.

Figuring out how ATTENDANCE worked took a few days—a little exploration in the computer, a little watching in classrooms. Every day the computer, the locked-away IBM machine, generated a list of students who were to be excused for arriving late to school. Each teacher got the printout in the morning. Paul now had the power to add any name he wanted to that printout and get a kid excused for missing a morning of school. Within a month Paul had made friends with a classmate nicknamed Psycho, a daredevil who took matters a step further by stealing the nurse's official notepad and ink stamp, which you could use to get excused in the middle of the day.

Paul's next computer program was a hangman game. It worked perfectly. His friends thought it was cool. But one day he dropped the punch cards that contained his game. Looking down at them scattered around his sneakers, he realized he hadn't numbered them. "Fuck this!" he yelled. His anger cooled eventually, but by then programming a computer seemed like something he'd already done. For years, until he got a machine of his own, he visited the computer room only to make arrangements for playing hooky.

As he had silently promised at convocation, Paul never did much homework at Boston Latin, except in eighth-grade physics. The teacher said no one would ever receive a perfect score in his class, and Paul felt so provoked he actually studied for the first test. He got every answer right, but the teacher, a notorious martinet, docked Paul a point for having left too much space between two words. Paul never made that mistake again. From then on he got hundreds on every test in that course. But none of his other teachers realized how easily he could be motivated. An A in physics and then it was back to doing the things he enjoyed—playing his trumpet in the school band; looking for used cars with Danny and their father, and scouring junkyards for brake rotors and carburetors; exploring Boston's subway tunnels with friends, squeezing against the walls when the trains went by.

Paul was industrious outside school. When Danny gave up his paper route, Paul took it over and managed two routes. In seventh grade, his first year at Latin, he took ten dollars of his paper route earnings and bought a dime bag of pot—from the same man in the North End who sold the boys fireworks. Paul sold the dime bag bit by bit and with the astonishing profit bought an ounce. In a corner of the attic he found a small munitions box that his father had brought home from World War II. He broke off the lock and bought a replacement at the drugstore, and he stored his drugs inside, mostly marijuana and also some mescaline. He hid the box in the eaves of the attic near his mattress. He never came close to getting caught. No one in the family knew, except for Danny, who didn't get involved and didn't tell, of course. Paul quit that business after about a year. He could have bought several used cars with his profits had he been old enough to get his driver's license. He returned to more conventional jobs during high school, working weekends at Medi-Mart and then at Lechmere Sales, rising in both jobs to the position of head cashier.

Long after his own career in crime had ended, Paul heard that Psycho had gone to prison for murder. Curious the difference in their trajectories, and tempting to imagine that it had been foretold in the difference between their Latin School thefts—Psycho's old-fashioned, Paul's ahead of its time.

When Paul invented his steal-the-teacher's-log-in ruse, the Internet was still just a small medium for specialists. The same genus of program would be invented elsewhere later on and become by the mid-1990s a favored and enduring ploy of online thieves, called phishing. Paul's program was an impressive little feat, considering its time and the equipment he used (already outdated in 1976) and the fact that it was the first program he ever wrote. He had a mind for the age that was coming. He stood on the right rung of the evolutionary ladder.

PART I

FORTUNES

1

THE ENGINEERING OFFICE OF THE KAYAK SOFTWARE CORPORATION
was murmurous. The collapsible walls that divided two of the conference rooms had just been moved aside, opening a theater barely large
enough to hold the voices and the hundred bodies crowding in. Paul
English stood behind a table, facing them.

He was tall, about six foot two, and no longer thin, though he
didn't look fat, just big. He had a prominent jaw and a large face that
in repose sometimes made one think of raptors, beaked with staring
eyes. He still had a boyish quality as well, along with all his hair—
dark with hints of Irish red, parted in the middle and curving slightly
upward to either side, like water rising from a fountain. It was November 2012. It had been more than thirty years since Paul had taken
Catholic Communion, and more than twenty since his last fistfight.
The skinny kid with a hot temper and an attitude now practiced
meditation. Traces of a Boston working-class accent still surfaced now
and then—"cahn't" for "can't," "drawr" for "draw," "remembah." And
he was still at risk of dropping what his assistant called "f-bombs" in

polite company. But these were like the fragments of a memory, buried under decades of experience and the transformations of success.

Paul had joined the world of software engineering some thirty years before, at a time when computers and software programs were becoming pervasive—an underlying part of everything, it seemed, and the source of a great deal of new commerce. It was the era that saw the rise of the personal computer, the Internet, the World Wide Web, the smartphone. An era with its own American success story, the story of the software entrepreneur, which begins in a garage instead of a log cabin. Capitalism had long depended on people with the ambition and daring—not to say greed and recklessness—to start their own companies. But lately, entrepreneurship had become a freshly exalted pursuit. It was a church, and Paul was now one of its bishops.

He was forty-nine. The crowd standing before him in the conference room was on average decades younger. Like most of them, he had been a computer programmer and by his own account uncomfortable in many social settings—or, as he put it, "shy." One engineer out there in the crowd remembered knowing Paul when they were both much younger, then seeing him again after losing touch for several years. "He seemed different," the engineer said. "He looked different, less nerdy. He seemed more cool."

Paul had worked at creating that kind of impression. At various times over the past ten years, for instance, he had asked fashion-conscious women friends to advise him on his wardrobe. He didn't feel that he had shed all his "shyness," but in this setting, anyway, he was a paragon of savoir faire. He had natural assets—his size, his prominent jaw, his hair. And here, of course, he was the boss.

When Paul was fired up, he spoke hyperbolically and very fast, dropping the *g*'s at the ends of words, eliding phrases so that they sounded like one word. But today his performance was muted. When the voices in the room had quieted, he said, in an offhand tone, which seemed strangely at odds with the message: "So I have a big announcement about the company that I want to tell you. We've actually agreed to merge with Priceline."

The crowd turned into doves. "*Ooooo*," they said.

Priceline was a large holding company of online travel agencies, and Kayak was a small and unusual but very profitable travel site. Until recently it had done no booking. Rather, it was a comprehensive search engine for travel, often described as "a Google" for finding flights and hotels and rental cars.

Paul and a young businessman named Steve Hafner had founded Kayak nine years ago, in 2004. Since then, many companies had offered to buy them out. But, Paul told the room, Priceline's offer was the only one with the right ingredients. First of all, the purchase price. "It's a one-point-eight-billion-dollar transaction," said Paul.

He made the translation: Kayak's stock was now worth $40 a share, $14 more than when the company had gone public four months ago, and $10 more than the current price. Paul didn't say this, but about half of the people on his team owned stock now worth at least $1 million, and some owned considerably more. Paul's was the largest take, some $120 million.

He didn't dwell on the money. Many of the newer faces out there in front of him owned little or no stock. And Kayak's lawyers had warned him not to say too much, lest he give ammunition to the lawyers who specialize in filing suits over the sales of big companies. Nuisance suits and regulatory agencies would probably delay the official closing of the deal, Paul said. In the meantime, things would go on here at Kayak just as usual. And not only in the meantime. This deal, Paul said, would put Kayak in position to become the strongest travel company in the United States and maybe even internationally. Priceline was rich and powerful. Its market capitalization was

$32 billion. And—this was the most important thing, along with the sale price—it had a history of letting its subsidiaries run with complete independence. He and his co-founder, Steve Hafner, had never wanted to work for anyone else, and this deal would preserve both their autonomy and the team's. "And I think we have a great team here. It's our team, it's our culture, we hire and fire as we want." There would be no layoffs. Kayak's managers wouldn't even have to attend regular meetings at Priceline. "I'm still here and signed up," Paul said. "Steve is still here and signed up."

He spoke these last words in a tone so different from his usual exuberance it made you wonder if he believed them himself. He didn't seem unhappy about the news he'd delivered—that Kayak, *their* creation, was now owned by a huge corporation—but he didn't seem in a mood to celebrate either.

Evening comes early in New England's November. The windows in the office were darkening by the time the meeting ended. Many of Paul's team, it appeared, couldn't wait to take the good news home. The team's most senior engineer had brought in a five-hundred-dollar bottle of Scotch, and several colleagues lingered in the aisles beside their desks, passing the bottle around. Paul sat at his computer, his broad back slightly hunched as he wrote "thank you" again and again to the congratulatory emails filling his screen.

2

PAUL HAD SITUATED KAYAK'S ENGINEERING OFFICE IN THE TOWN OF Concord, Massachusetts, just a few miles from the Old North Bridge, where the Revolutionary War began. But the immediate environs were a suburban office park, the kind of place you imagine being torn down even while it is being built. Paul almost always went in the back way, across a parking lot, into a brick building, up two flights of stairs, and through a gray metal door.

Business matters were handled by Steve Hafner in an office in Connecticut. The engineering office was Paul's creation and domain. It occupied two floors, all but identical and connected by a broad stairway. Paul and his architect had designed both floors in the open-room, tidy-industrial style: no private offices; conference rooms with glass walls; heating ducts and pipes left exposed in the high ceilings; everything gray or white with splashes of orange here and there. Most of the floors were filled with gray metal desks, arranged in complex, adjoining geometries. About a hundred people sat at them, in ergonomic office chairs, in front of large screen iMac computers. They could have been mistaken for a class of high school seniors, with a lot of thirty- and forty-year-old faculty mixed in. Only one was African American. There were many Asian faces and East Indian faces. Collectively, Paul's crew spoke twenty-one different languages. There was a smattering of women, three of them managers of teams and fourteen others carrying the title of engineer—a large percentage for a software company. The women were all better dressed than the men, who were a motley-looking bunch. Jeans and T-shirts predominated. Two engineers wore shorts and flip-flops in all seasons. There were shaved heads, beards, a ponytail, a funny hat with earmuffs. One fellow wore his pants too high for fashion anywhere outside a nursing home. Some were thin and pale as the winter light from their computer screens. Most were programmers. Looking across the sea of desks, Paul could pick out several dozen whom he affectionately described as odd—"on the spectrum somewhere."

He used the term loosely and with fellow feeling. He himself had been subject to a diagnosis: In his twenties, as a young programmer, he had been told that he suffered from "bipolar disorder." None of the young engineers at Kayak knew this, but the condition still loomed over him, and sometimes descended upon him. What his team did know about their boss was that he could seem like a force field of energy, and many if not all were drawn to that energy and lifted by it. At the same time, Paul had made this office into something like a bastion against the mad, work-all-night ethos that he had reveled in back in his own coding days—days of hundred-hour weeks. Kayak engineering was almost always empty on evenings and weekends. One new programmer who hadn't known any better and worked there all night had been told, when found out in the morning, "Well, okay. But go home soon."

Paul had arranged various amenities for his team: modernist paintings, which hung near the sofa where visitors sometimes awaited appointments; a kitchen with free drinks and snacks; two coffee bars with expensive espresso makers; a rec room with a foosball table and a pool table and a kegerator, available to anyone at any time but mainly used for "beer-thirty" on Friday afternoons. These perks were modest by the standards of established high-tech companies. On the other hand, the atmosphere at Concord seemed unusually informal. Some other companies in the software business, especially large successful ones, walled themselves in with their secrets, like dragons hoarding their gold and jewels. Here, there were no Keep Out signs on outer doors, no cameras patrolling the interior, no identity cards for employees to show to a scanner, and, for visitors, no nondisclosure forms to sign, not even a sign-in sheet.

Paul remembered the time when a young woman came to the front door and asked him for a job. She said she worked next door and through the walls it sounded as if a job at Kayak would be a lot more fun than hers. In fact, the atmosphere was congenial. There were parties, and members of Paul's team shared lunch and took breaks to chat with each other in the kitchen. Occasionally they called to each other from their desks. You didn't sense seething animosities. If any existed, they were subtle. Otherwise, Paul would have rid the office of them. He liked it that some of his team were boisterous extroverts. A few were given to practical jokes—wiring up a ballpoint pen so that it would shock anyone who tried to use it, and other proofs that some minds can race ahead without leaving middle school behind. But during most of the working day, when you looked across the sea of desks, what you usually saw were faces staring at computer screens.

These two rooms in Concord were Kayak's central factory, indeed most of what there was to the factory of a company that had just been sold for nearly two billion dollars. For many of an older generation, a sum like that evoked images of a vastly different industrial America, of factories like fortresses, of blast furnaces and vats of molten steel, of workmen with bulging forearms carrying lunch pails. Paul and some of his team were the children of such men, but for this generation, coffee break meant espresso.

Concord belonged to what was now a mighty segment of new American industry, mighty and yet utterly unmuscular-looking. A stranger walking into this office—a stranger who, like most of humanity, knew little about software—would have had to wonder what these eccentric-looking kids could possibly be doing to generate any money at all, let alone a fortune. Not for the stranger but for his team, Paul had tried to offer an answer. Programmers are always in danger of becoming happily abstracted from the consequences of their work. Paul had arranged to show his crew the fruits of their labor, a representation of their product's achievement—a representation in numbers, an abstraction itself.

A screen hung on each of the far walls of the second floor. One screen was large, big enough for an art house cinema. If you had looked up from your desk—say at 3:32 on the afternoon of November 7, 2012, the day before Kayak's sale was announced—you would have seen, in bold type at the center of either screen, this number:

2,737,926

Digits changed at stopwatch speed. Two seconds later the display read:

2,738,816

No explanation was provided, but everyone who worked here knew that this number represented the day's running tally of travel searches. The searches, that is, that visitors made between one midnight and the next on the Kayak website and the Kayak mobile application.

The display was old news now. You rarely saw anyone stop and stare at it, but seen afresh, it was mesmerizing. Mesmerizing just to watch the number grow, like fractions of seconds flying past—by midnight it would reach at least five million, and more than that during times of holiday travel. Paul had meant the number on display as a message to his team, his way of saying to them, "Good job. Let's do more." And it was also one of his ways of trying to put them in vicarious touch with customers. If you knew that the number at the center of the screen signified searches, it was bound to dawn on you that watching the digits grow was the same as watching millions of people typing at computers and swiping fingers over the screens of smartphones and electronic notepads as they brought up the Kayak website on their browsers and began to look for information about flights, hotels, rental cars. And you were also watching a machine at work, responding to all those people—a complex machine made out of software and silicon that was spread across a large part of the world, connecting millions *to* the world.

As the search numbers grew on the screen, you also began to understand Kayak's purchase price. The business worked this way: A user goes to the Kayak website, finds a desirable flight or hotel room or rental car, and then is sent to the website of an airline or hotel chain or car rental company, or to one of the online travel agencies, such as Expedia or Orbitz. Kayak receives a fee from those other companies just for the referral, seventy-five cents for a flight and two dollars for a hotel, and considerably more if the user actually books the car or the room or the flight through one of those other companies. So every number added to the tally of searches conducted on Kayak was like a sale rung up on a cash register. Advertisements on the site, demure by industry standards, added more. In the course of fiscal year 2012, Kayak's users made 1.2 billion searches. These brought commissions and ad revenues amounting to $292.7 million, and to profits of $65.8 million. Remarkable figures, not for their size but because only 205 employees had been required to produce them. In 2012, Kayak's revenues came to nearly $1.5 million per employee, one of the highest ratios among all publicly traded companies.

———————

How do entrepreneurs succeed? There is a form of business romance that says you must be "passionately" committed to your idea, your industry, your product. But what was there in Kayak's business to feel passionate about? Making sure that an ironing board was included in the first hotel room their website showed a traveler, or that a customer received accurate information about the prices and availability of seats on airplanes? Paul and his people cared about how to discover that a certain traveler was more apt to book a room with an ironing board than one without. They cared about delivering accurate flight information. (Not an easy or perfectible job, but well managed now by Kayak's six-member team of mathematicians and computer scientists.) And as a group, Paul's team cared about making the Kayak website produce, within seconds, an elegant-looking listing for that room or an accurate listing of flights between, say, Boston and Cleveland. They cared in part because doing those things increased the chances that customers would keep using Kayak and recommend it to their friends.

Mainly, though, Paul's team were craftspeople in software, employing the tools of logic—that is, approaching their tasks with a sensibility quite different from passion. One might infer the same about the spokeshavers and wheelwrights and blacksmiths and harness-makers of eighteenth-century Concord, who likely didn't care so much about travel itself as they did about creating the things, the wheels and wagons and horseshoes, that made travel possible.

Did anyone at Kayak feel passionate about optimizing a customer's flight options between Boston and Cleveland? If anyone did, it would have been Paul, but what he seemed to feel was empathy for customers—not passion but compassion. He had wanted everyone at Kayak—and especially the programmers—to imagine themselves in the place of that customer looking for the right flight to Cleveland. Paul had devised a scheme he called "Empath," which had obliged every coder in Concord to answer some angry emails from customers. All programmers were also supposed to take a turn now and then at answering the red phone. This was a big red plastic old-fashioned landline telephone with a very loud ring. Paul had bought it and had its number posted on the Kayak website, inviting customers to call with problems or complaints. "An angry customer is a passionate customer," he'd tell his team. "And if you can win them over, then you have a passionate advocate." He figured that if his engineers answered the emails and the phone, they would hear firsthand about problems, maybe problems that they themselves had created, and if they got yelled at by customers now and then—or, even better, had to listen to some customers cry—they would likely feel determined to find the guilty bugs as soon as possible and fix them

Eventually, Paul had given in and created a customer service team—paying people to care about the problems of strangers. The red phone still rang brassily, but only the senior engineer in charge of customer service could be counted on to answer it. And when he wasn't around, there was only Paul. He would let the phone ring awhile, hoping someone else would act. Then he'd make a dash for it, all but leaping over desks. Once he had a customer calmed down, he would say, "My name is Paul English and my email address is Paul at kayak.com. I'm actually one of the founders of Kayak." Sometimes he spent half an hour solving a customer's problem.

Travel was just something that Paul liked to do. What he really cared about was building new engineering teams. In a jaunty moment once, he said, "For me businesses exist as an excuse to get a team together, and product is what a team does. You have to pay salaries, so, unfortunately, you have to make a profit." Creating teams and managing them were his version of the business romance. He loved his own large biological family, he would say, but at times he felt as though at Kayak he was building another family, better in the sense that he could choose its members and fire those who didn't work out.

He used to have his own website, where from time to time he posted his algorithms for recruiting and hiring. He actually practiced some of the techniques he described. His usual pitch was seductive. In effect, he'd tell recruits that they had higher aims than simply making lots of money, and he'd congratulate them for it. High-tech America was vying fiercely for the best programmers and web designers. Paul could offer stock options and, eventually, competitive salaries, but all the people he hired could have made at least as much elsewhere. The extra thing he had to offer was his enthusiasm, aimed at recruits. He told them they were "awesome," "rock stars," "monster coders" who could "knock down buildings with code," and it seemed that in many cases both parties believed it.

Paul's recruiting might have served as the subject of a business school case study—called, let's say, "Why the Traits of Effective Leadership Can't Be Codified." A young engineer whom he had recruited to Kayak described Paul's courtship: "Maybe it's a technique, but within the first five minutes of meeting someone, Paul will tell them something personal: 'I broke up with my girlfriend last night,' or 'I was completely wasted.' It's disarming, especially if you know this is Paul English. Then you start to think of him as this empathetic being that you can totally relate to, and before you know it, you've totally fallen for him. I don't think people are loyal to him because of his innate managing ability. It's very stressful to work for him. He gets superemotional about stuff, and he changes his mind all the time. But ten minutes after meeting him, you think, 'I will follow that person.' And somehow that continues. People who make a strong first impression often pale, but not Paul. And I think it comes from knowing somehow he's someone you can trust and count on."

Recruiting and hiring were one of Paul's great loves, his knack for them perhaps his greatest pride. He hated firing people, though you would not have known that from reading some of his interviews in the business press. In the December 2010 issue of *Inc.* magazine, for instance, he was quoted as saying: "The only way 100 people can ever build a larger company than one that has more than 8,000 people— that's what Expedia has—is by hiring Olympic-quality, unbelievable all-stars of technology." To preserve that very high standard, firing people was also necessary, and not just a few: "I do all of the firing. At times, I've fired maybe one out of every three people I've hired. That might make people think I'm bad at hiring, but I think I'm quite good at hiring."

This sounded tough, and doubtless it was meant to. But Paul in action was more humanist than tyrant. According to one of his assistants from Kayak's early days, he once threw up in the bathroom the morning before a firing. He still offered to meet with each fired person outside of work. He would say, "It totally fucking sucks. I hate this. I have been fired myself. You can still be a rock star at some other company." Reassuring words for some perhaps, and dubious comfort for others, but he also tended to give the fired people very generous severance packages and to help them find other jobs. The first person he fired was a woman, a monster coder according to Paul, whom he had reluctantly let go. He said he once argued with her for an hour as to whether or not she was argumentative. Nine years later she seemed to feel that she and Paul together had decided she should leave. They were still correspondents and, she said, still friends.

Paul sometimes rated employees on the letter scale. He said he wanted an engineering office with nothing but As, and ideally he wanted A-pluses. On another occasion, though, musing about his engineers, he referred to one who was a solid but slow coder.

But hadn't he said he didn't allow Bs on his team? Why hadn't he fired that programmer?

Paul looked surprised. "But he's a great human being! He's a moral compass!"

Companies involved in computer technology often portrayed themselves as places of great liberality, as democratic and nonhierarchical. What this meant for employees, almost universally in the software business, was the freedom to dress as they pleased and to work odd hours—in some cases even from home. On other matters, meanwhile, the hierarchies of supposedly nonhierarchical companies typically went in for a lot of social engineering.

Paul had made it a habit to glance now and then through the transparent walls of Kayak's conference rooms, and, spotting meetings that he thought too large and long, he would poke his head in the door and with a smile, always a smile, say he was sure that three of the dozen people in there were smart enough to solve their problem in half the time they'd already spent. He also bought a tally clicker, a device that nightclub bouncers use to keep count of patrons, and hung it outside the door of the main conference room—this by way of saying, "I'm paying attention. I want meetings of three people, not ten." He also bought a toy stuffed elephant to be present at meetings, an embodied cliché, the elephant in the room. He named it Annabell. He had hoped it would encourage shy engineers to speak their minds to each other and to him.

Programmers tend to disdain titles, and at Kayak titles were deliberately meaningless. A solid engineer might be labeled "senior engineer" while an absolutely essential one, receiving handsome bonuses, might be simply called "software engineer" or "design architect." The person who should unquestionably have been called chief operating officer had given himself the nondescriptive title "senior vice president." His name was Paul Schwenk, known simply as "Schwenk" or "Papa Schwenk." The name fit him well enough. He was in his early forties, old enough to be the father of many here.

Since there were no private offices and the most senior engineers were scattered around on both floors, you couldn't read the hierarchy in the seating arrangements. But of course there was a hierarchy, and seating was carefully controlled, by Papa Schwenk and Paul. They wanted "the right balance of energy," Paul would explain. "We like people who are loud, but not right next to each other." At one point, Paul had dissolved his own favorite grouping, because he thought that he and the people seated around him were having too much noisy fun. Some engineers would get distracted if they had to sit too near the gregarious ones. Paul and Schwenk tried to assemble people whose tasks required them to talk to each other, but inevitably roles shifted and small clashes arose, so it wasn't at all uncommon for an engineer to come to work one morning and be told, "Schwenk moved you."

Once in a while, a programmer had resisted a new idea of Paul's, saying it was too difficult to implement. Paul had sometimes managed to get his way by saying to the recalcitrant coder, "Okay, but can you think of anyone who's smart enough to do it?" More often, though, he had let the matter drop. He didn't usually get deeply involved in technical matters. There had been some exceptions—most notably Kayak's UI, its user interface, the webpages that the site presented to customers' computers. In Kayak's very first days, Paul had made a survey of the other online travel websites, and to his delight he'd found them all to be slow, hard to navigate, and ugly, all jammed with enough garish colors to cause, as he liked to say, an epileptic fit. He wanted his team to create a user interface that was spare, elegant, and easy to use. To Paul, this meant it had to be fast.

To prove his point, he had the team create two versions of the Kayak website, identical except that one was half a second faster in responding to the user. The test subjects all declared that the faster version was simpler. "I don't want the user thinking about Kayak, but about hotels or flights. Speed allows that," Paul said. "I want a UI so simple that drunks can use it, with software so fast that someone who's ADD won't have time to be distracted away." He wanted the results of users' searches to be displayed on their computer screens within a hundred milliseconds. He took this request to his chief engineer, Bill O'Donnell, known as "Billo." For a time, Billo insisted the goal was unreasonable, even impossible. "Just try," Paul told him. Paul harped on the matter, and finally a concerted effort was launched, and rather to Billo's surprise, it worked.

In Kayak's first few years, when Paul had time to kill in airport waiting areas, he would look for people with empty seats beside them. He'd sit down and ask them to open the Kayak website on their computers. For what seemed like a long time, those strangers would ask, "What's Kayak?" And then, around 2007, the question began to change: "Kayak? You work there? You *do*?" The UI itself, Paul thought, had represented Kayak's first successful advertising campaign, the thing that had made people like the site well enough to tell their friends about it—free word-of-mouth advertising at last bringing customers to Kayak in profitable numbers.

The idea behind Kayak was undeniably clever and the timing good: When they started, there was no comprehensive and reliable search engine for travel, and a company that was just a search engine and didn't do booking didn't have to finance a large sales force and administrative apparatus. But the annals of American commerce are full of good ideas that failed. There is always some mystery, some concatenation of things, behind a success like Kayak's. Paul liked to say the company had flourished first of all because of abundant good luck, and because of his co-founder's brilliance. And also—maybe most of all—because of the engineering team.

In a business where not even powerful companies seemed to last for long, this intentional family of Paul's had unusual continuity. Six of the first dozen people he hired for Kayak had worked for him before—and not just briefly, but at five different companies over more than twenty years. His term for these people was "twenty-pluses." They still made up most of the engineering team's cadre. Among them, Papa Schwenk and Billo were preeminent. In Paul's lexicon, they weren't just "value-adds." They were "need-to-haves."

3

BILL O'DONNELL MANNED A DESK BESIDE AN AISLE ON THE OFFICE'S lower floor, a floor below Paul's station. You would find him sitting there working at his computer, short and stocky but fit, with a large face and thinning black hair, often dressed in a two-colored polo shirt—the sort of shirt you'd wear to a bowling league, Paul thought. Billo talked nearly as fast as Paul when he was telling a story or explaining something technical, but when he didn't have anything to say, he went quiet, and if you started to fill the silence with small talk, you were apt to find him staring at you, with no expression on his face. It was easy to imagine he was hoping you would hurry up and finish, or say something worth his commenting on. Not that he was rude, but especially when he was coding, you could stand in front of him for a very long time before he noticed you.

Paul said, "At some point everyone thinks Billo hates them." In fact, Billo was very popular, especially among Concord's young programmers. A young engineer named Vinayak Ranade told this story: "There was a guy I worked with that I never seemed to agree with.

We got along otherwise. We were just always at odds when it came to decisions about the product, and this was incredibly frustrating for me. As with everything, I ended up mentioning it to Billo. He said, 'If two smart and logical people disagree, it's most likely because they are acting on different information.'"

This proved to be true. Vinayak discovered that he and his colleague had been thinking about different issues, such as ad revenues versus customer complaints. Vinayak went on: "This is an example of why Billo's a great boss. In one sentence he distilled the root of my problem, showed me how to solve the problem, gave me a compliment. He didn't pretend that this was a teaching moment or that he was imparting great knowledge to me. He just told me exactly what I needed to hear at the right time. I started seeing all of my disagreements with the person in question in a different light. Since then, I've been applying this to a lot of conflict resolution or big decision situations at Kayak and even in my personal life."

Billo was a gifted manager, and it didn't hurt his popularity among the twenty-year-olds that at forty he still wrote a lot of code himself, and did so as fast and accurately as any of them. He came from New England computing royalty. His mother, the daughter of Italian immigrants, had run engineering divisions at two important Massachusetts computer companies—a rare feat for a woman. She had majored in math at Boston College and graduated as valedictorian of her class. Unlike her, Billo had always found math difficult, but it seemed to him that he had always known how to program computers.

Paul had discovered Billo's technical talent some twenty years before, when Billo had only recently graduated with a degree in computer science from Carnegie Mellon. At the time, Paul had become a manager of programmers at a large software company. When Paul had left that place to become a vice president at what looked like a hot new start-up, Billo had followed him. One reason was that for Billo, as for others, Paul represented something rare in the world of commercial software, an adept fellow programmer who could also deal with "the suits" in a company, shielding a programmer from the sorts of administrative and political folderol that most software engineers found dull or incomprehensible or both. Paul was also someone clearly on the rise, an engineer with dreams that could translate into both money and interesting new work. The time was the late 1990s. "There were Internet start-ups everywhere," Billo remembered. And Paul was very persuasive. He told Billo and some others that this new company—it was called NetCentric—was "a rocket ship."

It wasn't. "That place," Billo remembered, "was a clusterfuck of epic proportions. I wish I could teleport myself back to then and say, 'Get out!' I left quickly. Within two months. It was an incredible experience. A horrible commute. Insane start-up hours for ultimately no benefit, and my father died that spring. I just quit. I had no other job."

Billo took a break from Paul then, but within a year he returned, following Paul to two other companies, and finally, in January 2004, to Kayak. Paul wanted him to fill the role of Kayak's chief technical officer, the CTO. In keeping with local obfuscating practice, though, Paul took the title for himself, and Billo was called "chief architect," which was accurate enough, at least at the start.

When Paul first told him the idea behind Kayak, Billo said, "That sounds really boring." Moreover, joining up for Billo had meant taking a 50 percent cut in pay, at a time when his wife was pregnant with their third child. Why had Billo signed on? Partly, he said, he'd been persuaded of the commercial possibilities. "And," he added, "the fact that I would work with Paul on any idea that was viable."

Paul told Billo that he would assemble a technical team within two weeks, and within two weeks there was both a team and a place for them to work, a temporary office a few towns away from Concord. It was little more than a room outfitted with a large table where half a dozen engineers worked side by side, Billo first among equals. Paul had the dual gift, in the technical sphere at least, of identifying people he could trust and then of actually trusting them. He left it to Billo to manage the creation of Kayak's technology, and first of all the website's architecture—the blueprints, as it were, of a complex machine made of software programs and computers to run them. Billo remembered the job as deeply pleasurable, he and his colleagues at the table all knowing their roles, sharing a common purpose, combining into what he thought of as a "hive mind."

Their task was to create a website that contained a specialized search engine. At the simplest level, at what programmers call a high level of abstraction, the website would first take in a user's request— for example: Tell me all the flights from Boston to San Francisco and give me up-to-the-minute seat availability and prices. Then the internal software and hardware machinery would have to travel out, as it were, on the Internet and gather the answers from other websites and data banks, and filter the results, eliminating absurd itineraries— such as flights from Boston to San Francisco via Caracas. Then the machine would have to assemble a webpage of responses and present those to the user. And it would have to do all this very accurately and quickly, within a few minutes at most—and, if the site succeeded, do the same kind of thing over and over again, millions of times a day. "It's not floating-point nuclear simulations or anything like that," Billo would say of the chores the system had to perform. "But it does use a lot of computing."

Billo's little team had created many websites before and knew that they often broke down under the burden of early success, under the load of rapidly increasing traffic. In their talk at the table and the diagrams they scribbled, they imagined a system that was resistant to crashing and that could grow gracefully, a system that would "scale." Their plan didn't call for one gigantic program that would perform all the various required tasks. Instead, they broke the search engine into component parts, into about a dozen separate programs: a program that would search for flights, for instance, another that would check users' passwords.

These programs could be duplicated as many times as necessary to meet demand. The team aimed to keep all tasks discrete, so that the different software components of the search engine depended on each other as little as possible. Likewise the hardware, the computers. The discrete programs would run on many identical computers, the connections among them arranged so that if one machine broke down, another would automatically take over its work. As traffic grew, the whole search engine wouldn't have to be rebuilt but could simply be enlarged, by adding more copies of the various different programs and more computers to run them.

The start-up team worked fast. Within five months, by May 2004, they had created a functioning website. "It was actually pretty good," Billo remembered, in a voice that sounded mildly surprised. At the start, the system broke down periodically—first at around 1,000 visitors, then at about 10,000, finally at about 500,000. As the number of customers grew, the sheer amount of computing revealed bugs in the software. More often, bottlenecks developed in the databases. Fixing the problems usually took a few hours but always seemed to take forever, the engineers working feverishly, imagining customers out there in the world, staring at the interrupted searches on their computers, glowering at those rotating globes on their screens and vowing never to use Kayak again.

There were some memorable crises. On Christmas Eve 2006, the site suddenly couldn't handle the volume of incoming traffic and was teetering on the verge of breakdown. Fortunately, just a few weeks before, Billo had created a mechanism in the software that he called "lockdown mode," a figurative switch. He spent the night monitoring the computers in the system and when they started to become overloaded—"It's like a car engine that's lugging"—he would flip the lockdown switch. Users just arriving at the site would receive a message saying that the site was overly busy and asking them to try again in a few minutes. When people already inside the system were finished with their searches, Billo would reopen the site for a while and let some people in. "I was essentially standing at the door of a shop, letting customers in a few at a time when others left," Billo recalled.

The basic architecture of Kayak's site and internal search engine had survived, but over the years most of the software had been rewritten and its known flaws repaired. There were still only a dozen or so discrete programs running on Kayak's computers, but by 2012, at any given moment, there might be as many as four thousand copies of those programs running, communicating with each other and with Kayak's own very large databases situated in Massachusetts and Switzerland. And yet for some time now, Kayak's website had been up and running about 99 percent of all the hours in a year.

Both Paul and Billo kept abreast of changes in the online world, talking with colleagues, reading technical reports, trying out many new things. In 2008, when the smartphone was still a novelty, they both felt sure that mobile smartphone applications would supplement if not displace web-based sites on the commercial Internet. So Paul had asked Billo to put together a team and create a handheld version of Kayak, a version to run on smartphones and notepads. Billo had chosen three programmers for the job. The mobile app they'd created was a nearly instant hit. Kayak hadn't even tried to market it, but by late 2012 it had been downloaded thirty-five million times.

Paul rated Billo the best in the company in the purely technical sphere. Of Papa Schwenk, the chief operating officer without the title, Paul said, "Schwenk is killer. He is *the* most reliable person in the company. The businesspeople in Connecticut feel totally comfortable talking to him. Like he doesn't talk in gobbledygook? And he cares about them, like really cares about them, he wants to understand their jobs and he really listens to them. And the tech people all respect him. So on average Schwenk is the most respected in the company by the most people."

Schwenk was one of the first to arrive in the morning, right around seven, tall and thin, carrying his lunch in a brown paper bag. His gray mustache was always impeccably trimmed, his gray hair neatly parted in the middle. Add a tie and a starched high collar and he could have been a figure in a vintage photograph. He sat two dozen desks away from Billo, at the edge of the main aisle on the lower floor, an area of high traffic, a lot of it headed toward Schwenk. Not far away, another early arriver—a vice president named Jim Giza, another of Paul's twenty-pluses—would sit at his desk and listen with half an ear to Schwenk on the phone, solving problems for Kayak's European teams. "Norway, Lithuania, Berlin, Zurich," Giza said, "at seven in the morning they're all calling Schwenk. The flannel shirt, the beat-up pickup, you never would have thought he was the guy to hold it all together. Schwenk runs this organization, this engineering organization. Every kind of decision, from what kind of sodas do we get, to what kind of server do we buy, to who gets paid what—that's Schwenk. Paul comes in bouncing, bouncing, bouncing, and if he bounces up to me, I just bounce, too. Schwenk levels him. 'No, we're not spending eight thousand dollars on an exotic lamp, Paul.' 'No, we're not sending the entire company to the Bahamas.'"

Schwenk was raised in upstate New York. When he was still a

young boy, his stepfather moved the family to a run-down farm in the windy countryside, where they lived on food stamps and government cheese, and on the rabbits and squirrels and deer they managed to shoot. At dinner you didn't talk unless spoken to, and you ate everything on your plate, including the organs of the animals you'd killed, and Schwenk would say to himself, "I'll never let this happen to me when I grow up." Nor would he be cold, he thought, when at two o'clock on winter mornings he dutifully got out of bed and followed his breath, steaming in the frigid air, down to the basement to feed the homemade wood-burning furnace.

Unlike many programmers, Schwenk never fell in love with computers. He merely liked them well enough. For him, programming was fun but not something to get excited about. It had looked like a good way to earn a living. He went to the Rochester Institute of Technology on a scholarship and loans, and took his first job at Bell Labs in New Jersey, where he worked with scientists who knew nothing about computers and didn't want to learn. "They could barely turn one on. I like to say they were the smartest dumb people I ever met. They were super book-smart, but they had no common sense." Inevitably, he drew the contrast between them and the farmers around whom he'd grown up, who could find ways to solve whatever problems arose because they had to, for survival.

If Billo was chief mechanic, Schwenk was Kayak's farmer. Others knew more about how various parts of Kayak's technology worked, but only Billo and a few others knew more about all of it, and Schwenk also knew about everything else—what everything cost and where the revenues came from and who was sleeping with whom and who was working hard and who was wasting time playing video games and who was unhappy. You saw him everywhere around the office, moving not fast but purposefully, and usually willing to pause a moment to chat. Schwenk had assembled all the office chairs. It was Schwenk who crawled under the sink in the kitchen to clear a clogged drain, who called the plumber if he couldn't fix the problem himself.

He managed relations with the tax people and the finance people in Kayak's business office in Connecticut. He did all the budgeting and until fairly recently all the purchasing for Concord. In truth, he preferred to be in charge of expenditures: "'Cause I'm kind of, I don't trust many people? By my doing the budget, my doing the purchasing, I feel like, okay, it's under control, we're not going to spend a half million dollars for no reason."

Schwenk said, speaking of Kayak, "This is not a socialist or communist society." He said this, it seemed, by way of setting himself apart from Paul, who had fired people for good cause and then given them loans so they could exercise their options to buy Kayak stock at discounted prices. "It's insane," Schwenk said. "I would never do that." Certain jobs he performed alongside Paul—for instance, the periodic rankings of personnel and the decisions about bonuses. He spoke candidly to Paul about everything to do with Kayak, and he also managed Paul sometimes. "If I think Paul's email is stupid, I never answer it. Unless he asks again. Ninety-nine percent of the time he doesn't." This policy, generalized, had spread around the office: If Paul asks you to do something, wait until he asks you again. When Paul finally heard of this, he felt hurt, and then decided to take it as a compliment: His team didn't fear him.

Paul often talked about wanting to have engineers take risks and try new things, and at least some of the engineers took him at his word. Schwenk usually dealt with the consequences. He called this "chaos management." Suppose for instance that a team came up with a new webpage and put it online, and that this page happened to affect an existing business relationship—the placement of advertisements, perhaps, or the dispatching of an unusual number of users to one of the online travel agencies. Schwenk was the daemon, moving in the background, discovering the change, calling the affected parties, keeping the peace.

Billo and Schwenk. It was hard to imagine Kayak successful without them. They complemented each other at work, in their very different roles and their different ways—Billo often brisk and laconic, and Schwenk by comparison loquacious, maybe because he no longer wrote programs. They both were family men with children. Billo's wife was a doctor, Schwenk's a retired engineer. The two men rarely saw each other after work, and neither of them socialized much with Paul—partly because, unlike Paul, they didn't frequent clubs. From time to time both had found Paul exhausting, even exasperating. But they had both worked for him for most of their adult lives. In effect, they had bet on him, and the bet had paid off handsomely now. Paul had made sure that both owned Kayak stock in amounts commensurate with need-to-have status, stock now worth nearly $20 million for each.

Billo had prophesied something like this back in 1997, in the aftermath of the misadventure that Paul had led him on with the start-up company NetCentric. Schwenk had also followed Paul to NetCentric, and like Billo he had soon quit. Then the two of them had started their own little software company, along with an extraordinary programmer named Jeff Rago. But things hadn't gone much better with that enterprise than they had at NetCentric. Their idea was to build Internet-connected jukeboxes that would serve as advertising devices. The technology they created was first-rate, but it didn't sell.

"No money, no salaries," Billo remembered. "The sales guy we hooked up with was completely useless. No customers, no funding. A dump of an office, with a crappy old carpet, rummage sale furniture."

And then one day in 1998, Paul walked in. He was starting a new company, he told them, something called Boston Light Software.

Paul pitched the idea with his usual speed, his usual vigor and certainty. They'd build a website for building websites. He had a client already, he was assembling a team of old colleagues, getting the gang back together. Billo didn't say much, but as he listened, he thought, "This is going to work."

After Paul left, Billo told Schwenk and Rago, "Look, this thing's not going anywhere. We should go work at Paul's company."

They said they wanted to go on with their start-up.

"I feel bad leaving you guys," Billo told them. But he was going to follow Paul. Fifteen years later, he remembered his words exactly: "Someday this boy's going to get hit by a truck full of money, and I'm going to be standing beside him."

4

SCHWENK AND RAGO HAD SOON FOLLOWED BILLO AND PAUL TO
Boston Light, and about a year later, in 1999, Paul sold the company.
He gave half of his own proceeds to his team and still came away with
about eight million dollars.

Paul was only in his midthirties then. The most his father had
ever made in a year was fifty thousand, and Paul now had *eight million*. If you grew up in working-class Boston and you were a sensible
person, you wouldn't even let yourself fantasize about a windfall like
that. Who would have thought that rich people might struggle over
what to do with their money? He remembered thinking: *Growing up
we didn't have any money, so why do I get to have money? It just doesn't
feel right to me.*

In his childhood, rich people were as distant as movie stars and
baseball MVPs. Except that for as long as he could remember, he'd
been hearing about a man named Tom White. It was said that he
had been divorced, a thing both rare and shameful in the world of
Paul's Irish Catholic childhood, but he was also said to be a great

guy, who was very rich and gave a great deal of money to causes for the poor, and didn't want to get credit for it or even care to have it known. A lot of what Paul knew about Tom White came from Tom's nephew Mike, who was one of Paul's oldest friends. After his windfall, Paul called Mike and said, as he remembered the words: "You have this mysterious, elusive uncle who's a moneyman, right? Can you introduce him to me? I just made a bunch of money and I want to give a lot of it away." Paul felt as if he were a supplicant, all but begging for an audience.

Before the meeting, Paul did some research on the man. Tom— Thomas J. White—was born in 1920, grew up in Cambridge, attended the Cambridge Latin School and Harvard, then served in World War II as a junior army officer and aide to General Maxwell Taylor. He parachuted into Normandy the night before D-Day and later into Holland, and won a chestful of medals, including a Silver Star for valor. In the years afterward he took his father's moribund construction company and made it into the largest in Boston. He had been an intimate of the Kennedys, indeed JFK's chief political fundraiser in New England. He had been giving away money most of his adult life, beginning when he had only about a thousand dollars to his name. He had helped to found Partners In Health, well known for its work in medicine and public health in Haiti. Tom, it was reported, had donated $20 million to the organization.

Paul met him for lunch at the Riverbend Bar and Grill, in Newton. The man was eighty, with sandy hair going gray. He was small and slightly stooped, with a shuffling gait, a thin and slightly raspy voice, and a Boston accent not very different from Paul's. Paul liked old people. "They don't give a shit," he'd say. He meant that they tended to be forthright and free of vanity. And there was something especially disarming about this eighty-year-old, something that inspired Paul to play the wise guy with him. Maybe it lay in the figure

Tom cut in person, so unprepossessing compared to his résumé, or the fact that Paul had been hearing about him for so long that the man seemed almost like a relative. Forever afterward, Paul felt he could recite their opening conversation exactly.

"So I read about this group you're with, Partners In Health, that's been working in Haiti twenty years, and how you guys raised thirty million for it," said Paul. He added, "But twenty million, I heard, came from *you.*"

Tom blushed and looked down at his napkin. "Oh, I don't know about that."

Paul grinned at him. "I bet you think that makes you a good person. *I* think it makes you a shitty fundraiser."

The old man's smile sprang out so suddenly it startled Paul. Then Tom threw back his head and laughed at the ceiling.

For the next ten years, they met at least once a month. Occasionally they had lunch at Tom's country club, until the day Paul was stopped at the door because he was wearing blue jeans and Tom quit the club—largely on that account, he told Paul. More often they met at Tom's apartment in Cambridge. Tom would mix Paul a gin and tonic and they would talk, sometimes trading stories from their pasts. Tom had grown up in a three-decker in Cambridge, and he described his childhood as troubled. "We six kids were like six puppies. Children were definitely to be seen, but not heard," Tom wrote in a brief autobiography remarkable for its artlessness and candor. His father was a binge drinker. "He was not abusive to us, but it was as if we didn't exist. We never had family dinners except on major holidays and they were almost always a disaster because of his drinking. He once threw a holiday turkey right out the window. We never saw any affection between our parents. Never a good-bye kiss or holding hands—nothing." Tom remembered sitting with his sister trying to think of ways to create peace in the household. "Like all of my siblings, I grew up with a lousy self-image. I also felt it was my job to make everyone else happy (except myself). I survived but so did my sense of responsibility to try to make everyone else happy. I became the 'go to guy' for my family and, later in life, for many others. Even my mother used to say, 'You have a problem, see Tom.' I loved helping people except that at times it became quite overwhelming."

Paul said that he had grown up soaking in Catholicism. So had Tom. The experience had left Tom devout and Paul devoutly anti-clerical. On other scores, though, they shared a lot, including a psychiatrist, an elderly man named Jack Green.

Paul hadn't known of this connection. When it came to light, Dr. Green said that Tom had given him permission to tell Paul about their sessions. The doctor said that Tom often spoke about Paul during therapy, and often said how glad he was to have Paul as a friend. Evidently, Tom had been struggling with a bout of depression when Paul had first met him for lunch. "And you really helped him," said Dr. Green. Paul felt he had been handed an obligation, ill-defined but welcome, an obligation of affection.

He felt that he and Tom had become like brothers, and he also felt that in some ways they were like father and son. When he read the autobiography, it took him back to Tom's living room, and the pain in Tom's face when he talked about the homeless people begging on the corners around Harvard Square. Tom knew most of those people and their life stories, and he never left home without a wad of cash to distribute among them. One homeless woman told Tom that she would like to have a wagon to carry the bottles and cans that she collected for the deposits. The next day the aging tycoon was seen pulling a brand-new red wagon through Harvard Square to her corner. He gave much larger gifts to homeless programs and also to various charities, more than a hundred charities over the years. He did this partly for himself, he'd say: "I knew that one way to get rid of any depression was to do something for somebody else." He would also say that he'd learned there was no such thing as a self-made man, that all are born into conditions beyond their control, and that having money to give away to the unfortunate is a privilege born of lucky breaks.

Tom told Paul the stories about his first trip to Haiti, and how it had inspired him to finance the creation of Partners In Health. He told about the first time he saw a child with the symptoms of starvation, the reddish hair and bloated belly of what is known as kwashiorkor. "Put in a feeding program here," Tom had declared to the co-founders of PIH. He remembered encountering a child with big eyes and a memorable smile who was living in a dirt-floored hovel, and saying, "For Christ's sake, put a tin roof on and pour a concrete floor. I'll give you the money. Holy shit!" Speaking of his donations to Partners In Health, he told Paul much the same thing as he later wrote down: "I can't say that I never had a few qualms about giving but they were very few and as I went along I realized what great joy there was in seeing a child half dead and six months later seeing him running around having a good time with the other kids."

Paul didn't give away a great deal of the $8 million he got from Boston Light. After meeting Tom, he started writing $10,000 and $20,000 checks, mostly to organizations that Tom supported, mainly homeless shelters and Partners In Health. Later, after the founding of Kayak, the size of Paul's checks grew, however. PIH's chief fundraiser remembered the day in 2005 when Paul asked him to come over for breakfast, appeared at the door disheveled, and said, "I've been thinking things over and talking to Tom, and I'm going to give you a million bucks."

Over the next few years, Paul started running low on cash—he spent more than $2 million remodeling his house—but he borrowed against his shares in Kayak and went on donating money to his own and Tom's favorite causes.

Tom, meanwhile, was busy enacting a plan for self-impoverishment. He would say he didn't believe in "wearing a hair shirt" but had come to realize that stockpiling money was the equivalent of burying it, as a servant does in the parable of the talents. "I feel sorry for people that are wealthy and sitting there with millions—some of them billions—just making more money. I ask myself, 'For what?' Why don't they take a few million and give it to the very poor and marginalized people all over the world who suffer so much, in great part because of the greed of the wealthy?"

When Tom sold his Cambridge apartment and moved to a house in Newton, Paul felt bereft. He called Tom from Kayak and said, "Don't think you're going to get away without serving me gin and tonics. I'm gonna hunt you down and figure out where to get my drinks." An hour later, one of Paul's team came to his desk and told him there was someone at the door asking for him. It was a burly man in workingman's clothes, a tough-looking guy with a huge brown paper bag in his arms. He growled, "I'm lookin' for Paul English." He handed over the bag. In it Paul found seven bottles of gin, bottles of all sizes, from a nip to a gallon jug.

Tom was the person who made gifts. It could be hard to talk him into receiving one. One winter day, Tom's wife remarked to Paul that Tom would like to go to Florida but felt too old for all the rigamarole of a commercial flight. The next day Paul called Tom and said, "I went to this fundraiser and there was an auction and I won time on a corporate jet, but it's about to expire. Do you know anyone who could use it?"

Tom said, "You're full of shit," and hung up.

Paul redialed. "Tom, I didn't win it at a corporate auction, that may have been an exaggeration, but please will you let me fly you two to Florida?"

It took a while, but Tom eventually agreed. Then Paul called a friend in the aviation business, who told him he could rent a really nice jet for $18,000. Paul was aghast. He had entered his period of borrowing money. But he rented the jet and also a limo to take Tom to the airport, and just for the sake of Tom's company, he flew with him to Florida, returning the next day.

Tom had told Paul, among others, that once he had provided for his family's future, he would give the rest of his possessions away to worthy causes and die without a nickel of his own. By around 2009, Tom had been enacting this plan for most of a decade. He had grown very thin and frail, and full of worries. When he ran out of money, what would happen to the causes he had helped to finance? What would happen to Partners In Health?

By this time, Kayak was thriving, and Paul's stock had become a fortune, if only on paper. Paul told Tom not to worry. He would make sure that PIH didn't fail. "I don't have a hundred million dollars yet," Paul told him. "But I will."

Tom wasn't alive to see that day. He died at ninety, in January 2011—not penniless but close to it, Paul heard. Paul didn't have to rescue PIH, which had many other large donors by then, but he pledged to keep on giving money to the organization—another million once he had his Kayak winnings, and a hundred thousand a year for ten years after that. He had also joined the organization's board.

The year after Tom died, Haiti suffered its dreadful earthquake and ensuing cholera epidemic. When PIH's board was deliberating over ways to stanch it, Paul suggested that they use one of the expensive cholera vaccines, and then declared, "I'll backstop it." He added, "And let's vaccinate a hundred thousand people." Choosing a number simply because it sounded impressive was an old move of Paul's—"the big-number strategy." And it worked. It helped to get a vaccination campaign started, which helped to slow the epidemic and indirectly to increase the world's supply of cholera vaccine. In the end it cost Paul nothing, because the Red Cross ended up paying for the drugs. But the gesture—"I'll backstop it"—was one Tom would have made.

Paul's conscience had been affected by Tom, much in the way one's conscience is affected by one's father, by what one's father says and does. When Paul was asked why he wanted to give money away, you could hear something like an echo of Tom's voice, both in the quick reply—"What else would you do with it?"—and then in Paul's explanation: "I'm a little bit communist in that I don't think money ever really belongs to one person. Money's supposed to move around. I mean, money's a fiction, right? Money's this fictitious thing created to facilitate trade and for building things, so I think hoarding it is a disaster, because it goes against what money was created for."

Tom had agreed to let his name be put on a building only once—on PIH's Thomas J. White Tuberculosis Center in Haiti. Like Tom, Paul had been making most of his donations quietly, often anonymously. The boy who, like Tom, had felt it was his job to make peace in his childhood home had also, in recent years, become his own family's go-to guy. And since Tom's death, Paul had made repeated vows that he, too, would end up giving away everything he owned.

Often when Paul said this, he would add: "I just don't want to give it all away yet."

5

On November 9, 2012, the morning after the sale of Kayak was announced, Paul woke up to find his picture on the front page of *The Boston Globe*. "Priceline Makes a $1.8 Billion Deal for Kayak" read the headline. The caption added: "Kayak cofounder Paul English shaped apps that compare travel searches." All this in the newspaper that he used to deliver on his bicycle. In his place, of course, many hometown-boys-made-good would have been delighted. Paul felt like going into hiding.

Emails, texts, phone calls, even knockings on his door. All his channels of communication were flooded, less with congratulations now than with requests for money: pleas for help from pathetic-sounding strangers who might or might not be con artists; from old friends and new acquaintances representing worthy charities; from a doctor who had been treating him, now asking, on behalf of his hospital, if Paul would mind being contacted by the development office. Also from a friend of a friend who wondered whether Paul could spare fifty thousand for a real estate investment. The woman arrived at his door a few nights later, wearing a tennis dress though the night was chilly. Paul turned her down gently, simply saying that he didn't invest in things like real estate. He put off most of the petitioners by saying that he'd get back to them, that he didn't have any of his new fortune yet, which was true. His current therapist had warned him about giving money away recklessly. To resist seemed like the right thing to do, but it was painful saying no.

Like Tom, Paul had a knack for making money and didn't seem very interested in keeping it. Now he had an absurdity of money. True, some things remained out of his reach. He was still a member of that 99.995 percent of Americans who can't really afford a Gulfstream jet. But $120 million is exactly 120 times more than $1 million—a wholly different category of money for Paul, the kind of money that got one's picture on the front page of the *Globe*. Seeing his face there was like waking from a troubling dream, the dream of the unnamed crime. You wake up knowing you didn't do it, but the feeling lingers that you did.

When Paul first saw the article, his chest tightened, and it stayed that way as the emails and texts and calls kept coming. He had one main memory for explaining his discomfort, to himself and the therapists he'd seen over the years. He was five or six years old, and his ailing mother was in bed in the house on Perham Street, and his father was telling him and his six brothers and sisters that they were "all the same." Some of his siblings scarcely remembered this, and some thought their father had been trying to tell them they were all equally valued and also that none of them should get big heads. But Paul never heard his father's words that way. He felt his father was saying that Paul ought to *be* the same as everyone. His father's telling him not to make noise in the house—"You'll kill your mother"— meant that Paul should stop practicing the piano. Being *all the same* meant there might be something wrong in standing out, in trying to learn the piano at all, in trying to excel.

In a recurring fantasy, Paul was sitting in Tom's Cambridge apartment, drinking gin and tonics, and he was saying, "I made the big score, Tom. Let's figure out how to give it away."

It was too late for that. Without Tom to advise him, Paul went looking for substitutes. About a week and a half after the announcement of Kayak's sale, he drove to downtown Boston to visit a fellow member of the board of Partners In Health named Jack Connors. Jack was Boston born and bred like Paul, but a generation older and a great deal wealthier, a founding partner and former chairman of the huge advertising agency Hill Holliday. Jack had retired to a "family office," a suite of offices devoted mainly to his family's finances and charities, situated in the John Hancock Building. It is Boston's tallest building, and Jack's suite was at the top of it, on the sixtieth floor.

Paul arrived fifteen minutes early and lingered in the vestibule outside Jack's inner office. Paul was dressed like a construction foreman, in jeans and boots. He looked out of place and restive in the expensive stillness of the hallway, surrounded by blond wood and beige carpeting. At the end of the corridor stood a giant floor-to-ceiling window. He walked over to it. From that elevation, the landscape was a diminutive model of itself. Off in the distance he could make out shapes of real mountains, in New Hampshire presumably, and closer in, Boston's northern suburbs, and closer still, bridges, waterways, highways, railroad tracks, and finally, far down below his feet, the redbrick buildings and black-tarred roofs of the Back Bay. Gazing out was like looking at a painting, and Paul felt lost in it, until he realized again that he was looking through a window. Then he stepped back.

In this building windows had a notorious history. Soon after they were first installed, in the 1970s, they started falling out. Paul remembered the events well. He was probably seven years old when he saw the pictures in the *Globe* of the falling two-ton sheets of glass. No one had been injured yet, the paper said, but Paul felt so worried that someone would be killed that he set about trying to figure out the problem, and then, once he thought he had the answer, he felt even more worried. Maybe the owners of the building didn't know what was wrong. So he wrote a letter to the president of the John Hancock insurance company, explaining that metal and glass expand and contract at different rates, as his father had taught him. Not very long afterward Paul received a letter from the company's president, thanking him for his concern, and also a large book about the U.S. presidents.

When Jack Connors appeared, he greeted Paul with a firm handshake and a hearty slap on the shoulder. Jack was gray-haired and short, at least compared to Paul, and he was impeccably dressed, in slacks and jacket and necktie. He didn't comment on Paul's jeans and boots; the older generation of suit-and-tie America had long since learned to tolerate techie informality.

In the Kayak engineering office, Paul seemed always in command, even when he was being teased and contradicted. Now, sitting on a sofa inside Jack's office, his words came fast but disjointedly. He kept touching his chin and lower lip as he talked. "And it's been awful and I, basically, I need to think about how I plan my next decades and how can I use this money and how do I say no to people," he said. "Every nonprofit you can imagine sent me emails: Oh, what good news, we'll meet you for coffee. Every five minutes I get these and I've literally had chest pains since last week and I need to start, it'll probably take me a year, I just need to put a plan together how I'm going to deal with this."

In a calmer moment Paul could easily have given himself the advice that Jack administered: Get a lawyer, get a buffer between your money and your supplicants, above all take your time. But sometimes you can hear sane counsel only if it comes from a disinterested party, in this case someone Paul could count on not to need his money.

The ride down in the elevator was so smooth and swift that it seemed as though there was no transition between Jack's aerie and the street, where the demented Boston drivers were making the usual ruckus with their horns and a man dressed in jeans had many compatriots. Walking to his car, Paul talked about how uncomfortable he often felt at fundraisers for Partners In Health's work in Haiti, where "rich people" got dressed up and talked about the poor. *Rich people.* He used the term as if he still didn't believe he was one of them.

PART II

———◆———

THE FIRE

1

A WEEK AFTER HIS MEETING WITH JACK CONNORS, PAUL SAID IN A musing tone, "Money. There's a degree to which it's a burden and a responsibility. But mostly it's nice." Clearly, he was reassured by the spirit of Jack's counsel. He followed only some of it. He tried the buffer strategy briefly and found it didn't suit him. But he did employ the advice about taking his time. He put Kayak stock worth $40 million into an irrevocable charitable trust and resolved not to worry for the time being about making a plan to give the money away. No doubt this was wise of him, given the rate at which his life was speeding up.

You didn't have to be around Paul long to get a taste of his vigor. He didn't walk so much as stride, moving so quickly that it was hard to keep up without performing a combination of jogging and race-walking. His speech could accelerate to the point where you had to strain to understand him. He tended to repeat himself, telling the same stories to the same person, forgetting he had told them. To many of the people around him, all this was "just Paul"—an energetic, confident, talented guy who happened to be "hyperactive." But in Paul's case, hyperactivity was likely just a symptom of his deeper problem, his "bipolar disorder."

The general term denotes what used to be called manic-depressive illness, now broadened to include intermittent, alternating, and sometimes mixed states of depression and mania, varying widely in kind and severity. In the past, Paul had suffered from near-immobilizing depression but not from the psychotic states of full-fledged mania, in which one is consumed by delusions. He was subject instead to the oddly, vaguely named "hypomania," which means less than full-fledged mania.

"The labels are kind of dumb and meaningless, because no one really knows how the mind works," Paul once said. "What's really important is, what are the symptoms you're having that are bad? And then, what things can we do to make those symptoms be less?" He and his current psychiatrist had found a drug, an antiepileptic called Lamictal, that had kept Paul's depressions mostly at bay for a decade, and with minimal side effects. But his bouts of hypomania, his "highs," recurred. At their apex—when he felt "on fire"—he was prone to what psychiatrists and therapists call "grandiosity." Then everything seemed possible for him and the success of every new venture assured. A hypomanic high could also be a lonely and irritable state, as when everyone seemed too slow to understand him and he'd stare at people who were talking to him, straining to be polite. "That's pretty funny," he would say, while thinking, *You just made my blood pressure go up, because I just lost three seconds that I'm going to beg for on my deathbed.* Often during highs, he gave away a lot of money. More important, he scarcely rested and sometimes used alcohol to calm himself, and a high could lead to his sleeping with someone he later felt he shouldn't have. When he returned to a quieter state, his fires banked for a while, these risks were clear: "It's bad for money and sex and for drinking."

But as a rule hypomania took away his ability to resist it, even when he was aware of being in its grip and mindful of the risks. In Paul the highs tended to build in intensity, sometimes over hours, sometimes, it seemed, over months. Usually, a set of physical sensations told him the full-blown thing was arriving. He would feel a tingling in his arms and hands, then blood racing through his arteries and veins. The colors around him changed, sometimes to lurid hues, and he felt alert to everything. He was reminded of the commotion of feelings that came flooding over him in the moments before a traffic accident. But the sensations around accidents soon subsided. These lasted for hours, sometimes for days, rising and ebbing and rising again. The overall feeling struck him as bizarre, as something that his body wasn't meant to feel. An uncomfortable state when he'd first experienced it years before. Now when he sensed it coming, he felt both a little frightened and thoroughly exhilarated. In one email, he wrote: "Adrenaline. Hard to sit. Mind racing. Thrill. It feels good." In another: "If someone invented a drug that normal people could take to feel like i feel this morning, that inventor would be a billionaire." On one occasion, he said, "I *love* the highs. I can feel the blood racing through my veins. And I get a lot done." In the midst of a high, he was apt to wonder what it was that needed to be cured. He knew this in his quieter times: "It's a funny thing about mania—it feels so good that when it is with us, we feel cured, perfect, and we don't want the meds anymore."

Paul no longer hid his diagnosis, but he didn't advertise it either, and he wasn't always in its thrall, or disabled when he was. During the nine years he'd spent at Kayak, there had been times when he was in and out of hypomania and had managed to focus intently on the company. There had also been times when he'd been in the same alternating state and had applied himself to Kayak and many lesser projects at once. He began doing this now, in the early winter of 2013. It was a period when time around him seemed oddly shaped, many things continuing, many dying, many beginning.

His days ended late and began early. He never watched TV when he was alone, and he rarely slept more than four hours. So, by his calculations, he had the advantage of five more waking hours than most people. Often he woke to find a new idea waiting in the doorway of his consciousness. The hours before dawn were times of freedom, when he hadn't yet remembered all the meetings of the day to come and he could roll over and grab the notebook he kept by his bed and jot down an idea that had hatched in the dark. Some ideas never made it to daylight. Some he liked well enough to bequeath to friends, in emails with time stamps such as 4:15 or 5:03 A.M. For example, this offering sent to a former boss, now on the board of Procter & Gamble:

> Scott—here's a wacky product idea for P&G—
> The Calendar Toothbrush Package
> This is just 12 toothbrushes, but each one with the name of a month on it. This simply reminds the consumer to change their toothbrush every month.

Some ideas came contained in dreams. Some were pictures, and he would draw them in his notebook—the design of a new cupola for the roof of his house, the outline of a new webpage to show a UI designer at Kayak.

He had been divorced for most of a decade. He and his ex-wife remained on friendly terms and shared the parenting of their children, one in high school now, the other in college. There was only one woman who might have been called a near-constant presence in his life these days, but, as often happened, she had recently broken up with him. In her absence, one was aware of various other women passing through his life. He described all of them as "beautiful" or, what meant the same thing, "ridiculous." There was a black-haired dancer; a publicist with coffee-colored skin and a cinematic face; a nurse with a contagious laugh, who worked in poor and distant countries; a young executive seldom without a cellphone at her ear, who talked even faster than Paul and loved a noisy argument. There were the two sisters who dined together with Paul at a restaurant one night—something was said that made the sisters look at each other, then leave for the ladies' room together, and the rest of dinner was uncomfortable and didn't last long.

In November 2012, around the time of Kayak's sale, Paul had spent parts of many days at the office in Concord, including one whole day in raucous meetings with various members of his team. Meetings about "smartys," "pills," "APRs," "mocks," and other items of web design, Paul more or less presiding but everyone talking fast, everyone interrupting everyone else, including Paul, data flying around the conference rooms like bullets. (Who knew that the Swiss tend to drive to Germany for flights, because fares are cheaper there?) Paul went home exulting: "I had a *blast* at work today."

Then one morning in December, he awoke thinking that Kayak's engineering office should probably be moved from Concord to Cambridge. A few nights later, the perfect new office appeared to him in a dream, and when he woke he wrote up the details and sent them to his favorite architect. The items included a "dynamic video wall," which would be different from all other video walls, a video wall, Paul said, worthy of being shown at Boston's Institute of Contemporary Art.

Another morning he awoke to two ideas contained in dreams. One had to do with Kayak, the other with a refinement to a project he called Road Wars. And then it was out into the waking world, out onto the roads of Boston and its suburbs, heading to meetings on half a dozen different subjects, most of which had nothing to do with Kayak. On the way, between phone calls, he played Road Wars. It was a smartphone driving game that he had invented and was paying several friends to program. Your smartphone kept track of the roads you traveled and their speed limits. You conquered roads by driving safely over them. You lost points for speeding and for making or receiving texts and phone calls while you drove. The game hadn't been released to the public, but he and half a dozen friends were running trial versions, competing ardently. He said the game was mainly designed for teenage drivers, to beguile them away from bad driving habits. He thought he himself might benefit. Over the past thirty years he had accumulated some seventy moving violations. He still got a ticket now and then.

For years, Paul had been practicing Buddhist meditation. He meditated on weekdays when he could, and always on weekends. Sometimes he meditated in the car. One evening in the late fall, caught out at rush hour, surrounded by unhappiness—tired, bored, and angry faces, blaring horns—he smiled toward his windshield and quoted Thich Nhat Hanh's advice, that one should calm oneself in traffic by imagining the smiling eyes of Buddha in the red brake lights ahead. "This is awesome," Paul said. "That I get to *not* hit the car in front of me. I have a safe buffer. I need to be so many feet from him. It feels good. Then there's the stoplight. I'm not moving, so I can look around. I look for grass and flowers and light and sometimes people. I don't think most people look at grass. I *really* enjoy it. I think you enjoy something if you practice doing it. And that's what mindfulness is all about."

He lectured on entrepreneurship, each performance a potential recruiting session, at the Rhode Island School of Design and Northeastern University, Harvard Business School and MIT's Sloan School of Management. He presided over Tuesday Night Dinner, TND, held at his house and open to any of his siblings who cared to come, and always to an elderly former engineer, a widower who lived alone next door. There was party planning. Paul maintained a Google document where he recorded the details of his big summer party, Shake the Lake—a tent, abundant drink and food, including in some years a pig roast, a gigantic slip 'n' slide (a sort of sledding hill greased with soap and water, especially alluring to children and inebriated adults), a variety of bands and vocalists, and every year a new special feature (last year hula-hoop lessons from two young women in short skirts). Many days, he went to five or six meetings at different sites: to advise a struggling programmer at Partners In Health; to have lunch with his famous friend Sir Tim Berners-Lee, who had developed the software behind the World Wide Web and, rather than try to gain from it, had given it to the world. There was always email, a legitimate message arriving every five minutes on average. He visited venture capitalists with an eminent doctor friend in tow. The doctor had an idea to create a Kayak-like search engine for medical services—to create an online "health marketplace." At one meeting Paul remarked, "I'll pick the CTO, or, under some scenarios, *be* the CTO."

He was also trying to start two new philanthropic projects. Partners In Tech would support the work of Partners In Health: "It could be everything from someone's building a clinic, to providing Skype and Internet and mobile phones for community health workers in Haiti." He called, emailed, and visited fellow entrepreneurs, asking them to contribute—to no avail so far.

He started his most ambitious civic project in late December, not long after Kayak's sale was announced. It began when he heard the news of the slaughter of schoolchildren in Newtown, Connecticut. Afterward, he listened on the radio to the National Rifle Association's official response. It was the usual defense of a dangerous technology; no blame ever attaches to things, just to people. More guns in the schools was the NRA's solution.

The next day, Paul sat at his desk in Concord, muttering with a reddened face about the dead schoolkids, about the NRA and America's insane gun culture. On the following morning, various friends of his found a Google document in their email. It was time-stamped 5:09 A.M. and labeled "Preliminary." It announced the creation of something called the American Gun League, the AGL. It read:

> The AGL is a new 501(c)(3) association of American gun owners who believe in common sense laws for gun safety. The AGL will become the other seat at the table (other than the NRA) at all national discussions of gun owner policy positions and changes to gun laws.

Paul seemed to suggest amazing progress already: "We are raising millions of dollars and are forming a team of nationally known military leaders and celebrities and we will be backed by pro-bono work by top marketing, legal and social media companies." He closed: "Others have created alternatives to the NRA, but all of them have sucked in terms of brand. Ours won't suck."

The idea seemed rational, but the fact was that the AGL didn't actually have 501(c)(3) status yet, and not a penny had been raised from anyone, nor had any military leaders or celebrities joined the nonexistent board.

In the days and weeks that followed, the pace of Paul's life seemed to accelerate. It wasn't an increase in the fullness of his days, already packed, but a rise in their pitch, as if there were an ever-swelling soundtrack accompanying him. You could hear the brass when he spoke up at meetings he convened—in Boston, New York, and Washington—to create the AGL: "This is fun, taking out assholes." "I bet the NRA doesn't have any idea what's about to be unleashed on them." "I'm going to go to my billionaire friends and say, Dude, you need to give one percent." He told one AGL planning meeting that at Kayak they had competed successfully with the company Expedia. "But the NRA's tougher than Expedia. Expedia doesn't have guns." You sensed that he was trying to make this challenge more inviting for himself. As if it weren't daunting enough already—to take on one of the most successful pressure groups in American history, a group that was lavishly funded, clever, ruthless, single-minded.

"Do you agree with one of my interim goals, ten million members?" he asked an ally at another AGL meeting. Then he added, in a tone that made it sound as if he really thought he was being cautious: "Maybe five million is enough."

The New Year holiday came and went. It had been weeks since Paul had talked about his tech fund for international health. On a January morning in 2013, he dreamed that it was light outside and awoke to see his windows dark at five, and was surprised to see it was still winter. That evening, driving home in the early darkness, he turned off Road Wars so as not to lose points for cellphone use, and made a brief phone call to a person he'd been recruiting to help create the Kayak-like medical search engine. "I'm really reckless in entrepreneurship," he said over the phone as he drove. "I'm not saying that's a good way to do things, but this isn't moving fast enough." Just like that, he killed a project months in the planning. Then he turned Road Wars on again. In the latest round of competition, Paul was in second place, which was unacceptable. And so—saying, "Exxon-Mobil should be my sponsor"—he left the highway much sooner than usual and took a very long way home, amassing roads and bonus points, his phone, mounted on the dash, acknowledging his gains— emitting the sound of coins cascading from a slot machine.

Back in November, when Kayak's sale was made public, Paul had said wistfully, "As of tomorrow morning when I wake up, I'm now an employee." Since then, he had given some bursts of energy to this new role, but it had been weeks since he had talked about finding a new office in Cambridge for Kayak, or about the "video wall," or about much of anything else to do with Kayak, except to say, "I have to show my face there once in a while."

Then, one morning, he drove out to Concord to give one of Kayak's vice presidents a routine quarterly evaluation. They settled down in the conference room that was home to the stuffed elephant, Annabell. Then the VP, taking the embodied message to heart, asked Paul, "Can I give *you* some feedback?"

"Sure," Paul said.

"How many hours a week do you work at Kayak lately?"

"I don't know," said Paul. "Twenty?"

"Try three," said the vice president.

Paul didn't believe it, not at first. But when he looked around the office, he realized to his dismay that there were new young people there whom he didn't know. Whose names he didn't even know! When and how could this have happened?

It took him three weeks to act.

2

PAUL LIVED ALONE, IN A HOUSE JUST OFF A HEAVILY TRAVELED, tree-lined street in the colonial town of Arlington, ten miles northwest of downtown Boston. No gates or high walls or security cameras stood guard around his house. It was old, but Paul's extensive renovations had included many half-hidden features, such as the outside wall that could be rolled aside, opening the house's arms for guests at summer parties. He had bought the place mainly for its setting, half an acre of lawn running down to the edge of a large pond, called Spy Pond. He had equipped the house with a lot of technology: a huge, seldom-watched TV; automated lighting and heating gizmos that he could control with his smartphone; an elaborate sound system. But the house retained some of its old-fashioned self, with its ells, steep roof, and clapboarded walls, and the general lack of ostentation inside.

He had an office at the far end of the house, but sometimes, as on a night in early February, he carried one of his big, sleek computers out to the dining room. He worked there on email for a while, the computer's keyboard clicking fast under his fingers, a sound like distant surf. Then that sound stopped, and in a moment the machine began emitting little whoops, like a baby's digestive sounds— the sound of instant messages being sent and received. "This is a pretty momentous IM for me," Paul said, staring at the screen.

A conversation was unfolding there, Paul conversing with Steve Hafner. They typed their messages in lowercase and texting shorthand ("y" meaning "yes," for instance). Paul had begun the exchange:

"hey"

"yo"

"can i type conf?"

"y"

"so i'm bored"

"i know"

"if i leave, is there anytime better than another?"

This went on awhile, Steve asking Paul to help him with the transition and Paul writing that he would "love to continue a role" at Kayak. Near the end, Paul wrote: "also, i have no idea what i want to do next."

What he did next, as soon as he signed off, was to put in a phone call to Billo. Paul told him: "I just want to let you know that I told Hafner that I probably want to leave Kayak in a couple of months. . . . In a nutshell I'm not sure what I want to do next. . . . And just to say I'd love to find a way to work with you again at some point."

Billo said he felt the same way, and Paul hung up. His mind was moving fast. He called Schwenk and told him he was leaving Kayak. "We have to figure out how to reorganize Concord. I have some ideas. The other thing is, I'd love to work with you again. No idea what."

When that call ended, Paul said, of Schwenk, "He wants in." Paul was grinning. Starting a new company with Billo and Schwenk would be *awesome*. "It would get such attention in the industry. Any venture capital firm would give us five million, no questions asked."

A moment ago he had told Hafner and Billo he didn't know what he'd do next. If that had been true, it wasn't any longer. He would create an incubator. This was the common term for an entity that helps entrepreneurs turn start-ups into actual companies, usually lending them advice and office space and sometimes money, in return for part ownership in the new enterprises. "There are lots of incubators. But I don't care." Seated in front of his computer but looking off toward nothing in particular, Paul went on, "If I did an incubator, here's what the building would be like. It's a four-story building in Boston. The fourth floor is for me and the Kayak guys. Let's say it's called Blade Boston. That would be the badass, elite, best engineering team in Boston. We do our own things but we also advise. You have to make formal application to become a member. If you make it in, you get: One, free real estate for a year. Two, I take ten percent of your company. Three, we help them with strategy, production, architecture, and financing, and once they get financing, we kick 'em out. It's a four-story building. Floor one has a small kitchen, a small smoothie bar, a personal trainer room. Mind and body. It might be open to anyone in the tech Boston Blade community. There would be classes. The basement is a speakeasy, like from the 1920s. It would be public. And there would be an illegal private club on the roof, with a hot tub, pool, amazing sound system, and lights. I'd give it to my friends to use, with two requirements, that my bartender has to work it and my DJ . . ."

In his phone call, Paul had asked Billo and Schwenk if the three of them could meet for lunch the next day. Paul chose a place in Lexington, far enough from Kayak's office in Concord that no one from work was apt to be there. He told his two lieutenants what he had in mind: an incubator that wouldn't be called an incubator because most of those fail, but which would nurture start-up e-commerce companies that the three of them felt were promising. "Give them free room and advice and take ten percent of the equity, then get them financing and kick 'em out."

"It would be a little holding company?" asked Schwenk.

"We put our own money in?" asked Billo.

"We have the choice," said Paul. "We'll shape them and improve them, then flip them to a VC. One of us then joins the board." He added, "I'm thinking of calling it Blade, but I'm open to other names as well."

It was a vague plan, almost a plan without a plan. But all three had the safety net of millions in the bank. They could withstand a failure.

"I could do it for a while," said Schwenk.

"So could I, without hitting the college or retirement nest eggs," said Billo. "I could totally do that."

"Yup, I'm interested," said Schwenk.

"Yeah," said Billo. "It sounds very exciting."

Schwenk looked thoughtful. "My only concern is not having enough to do. I don't think I can code anymore."

"Sure you can," said Billo. "It's riding a bike."

Just like that, the matter seemed settled. Briefly, they worried aloud about the consequences for Kayak. Once the sale to Priceline was officially closed, Kayak would, as promised, remain an all but independent entity. Paul and Billo and Schwenk all agreed that they would have to arrange a transition in Concord's leadership.

And then the tea and coffee came, and for a moment they reminisced, three old colleagues around a campfire. All three were still in their forties. They all looked in good shape but too old for starting companies—that is, according to the current legend, which had it that old age began when you started shaving.

"We started Kayak in our thirties," said Billo. "We thought we were so old."

"I was forty-one, I think," said Paul.

Schwenk said, "I can't imagine another nine-year project."

"Neither can I," said Paul. "But we could have flipped Kayak much sooner. . . ." His voice trailed off.

Outside, in the pale, sunless winter air, on the gray suburban street, the world seemed drained of all color, but Paul was immune to dreariness just then. "That went well for me," he said as he started his car, adding, "That was highly emotive for Billo." Then he was musing out his windshield: "I'm going to sweep people in over the next few months with my enthusiasm. I could totally do it without Kayak people, but Billo and Schwenk and I have worked together a long time."

He concluded, "Last night I resigned, and today I'm pitching something new. It's an exciting time for me."

Two days later, Paul wrote up a document, time-stamped at a little after four in the morning:

Blade incubator requirements

1. Space for 12 engineers (core team) expansion possibility for up to 30.
2. Maybe ~ 150 square feet per engineer (?)—thus spaces from 2,000 to 5,000 square feet?

3. Walk to MBTA.

4. A dozen restaurants and bars within a block or two.

5. Very hip feel. Distinctive from the street.

6. Very open space.

7. Move-in date June 2013 or sooner.

8. Lease or purchase options considered.

9. Parking options to be discussed.

PART III

A SMALL UNIVERSE

1

ONE IS ALWAYS AWARE THAT INDIVIDUAL TALENT GETS SUPPRESSED by societies, the gifted child mired in poverty. But there may also be a kind of talent that gets suppressed by time, a talent diffused within the human gene pool, which lies dormant awaiting its technological moment. One of the fathers of computer science, Donald E. Knuth, speculates that this was the case with computer programming. In a series of interviews published in *Companion to the Papers of Donald Knuth*, he is quoted as saying:

> I've noticed that one out of every fifty people, more or less, has the peculiar way of thinking that makes them resonate with computers. Long ago, such people were scattered among many other disciplines, which didn't quite suit their abilities, but they discovered each other when computer science was established as a separate field.
>
> I mean, I think it's likely that one out of every fifty people who built the pyramids, ages ago, would probably have

been a great programmer if computers had existed in ancient Egypt.

In another conversation, Knuth refers to these born programmers as "geeks." This used to be the name for carnival performers portraying wild men, but it had long since been reapplied to denote socially graceless eccentrics who might also be dedicated to a special field. More recently, it had also become a term of proud self-mockery. Knuth used it that way:

> For simplicity, let me say that people like me are "geeks," and that geeks comprise about 2% of the world's population. I know of no explanation for the rapid rise of academic computer science departments—which went from zero to one at virtually every college and university between 1965 and 1975—except that they provided a long-needed home where geeks could work together. Similarly, I know of no good explanation for the failure of many unsuccessful software projects that I've witnessed over the years, except for the hypothesis that they were not entrusted to geeks.

In 2015, Knuth was a professor emeritus at Stanford. Oddly enough, way back in 1990, he had abandoned his public email address. There were several other ways of reaching him, which he had described on the Stanford University Computer Science website. You could use "good ol' snail mail," which he would deal with collectively, "in batch mode—like, one day every three months." You could also fax him. "But be warned that I look at incoming fax mail *last,* perhaps only once every six months instead of three." And you could *try* emailing him, via a couple of special impersonal addresses, but he would not answer any unsolicited emails, except for those that reported errors in his books.

All this suggested a most antisocial fellow, a Dickensian character who informs his public, "You can reach me by carrier pigeon, or, less reliably, by messages in bottles." But one could sympathize. He was in his seventies now and trying to finish *The Art of Computer Programming*, a work of seven volumes. He had begun to write it in 1962. In 2015, he was living on one of Stanford's quiet residential streets, in a house that he and his wife had helped to design—he'd had a pipe organ installed in one of its rooms; he was a fine amateur musician. He spent long hours in his home office, creating drafts of Volume 4B of his gigantic book. That volume alone had grown, in concert with the rapidly expanding field it explored, to three lengthy volumes of its own, only one of which was finished. As he explained on the Stanford webpage, the work he faced was the kind that requires "long hours of studying and uninterruptible concentration."

It wasn't as if Knuth forswore communication with the world. He just wanted to do it on his own terms. Though he no longer taught regular classes at Stanford, he still gave half a dozen lectures a year. He played the pipe organ at his church (Lutheran), and, at least in the past, he had led a Bible study class. Over the years, his work had obliged him to confer with thousands of colleagues, and he welcomed readers who identified errors or made "significant suggestions."

Knuth had received more than a hundred honors and awards, including the most prestigious available to computer scientists. These came mainly because of the first three volumes of *The Art of Computer Programming*. Those 2,200 pages had brought the rigor of analysis and mathematical proof to computer algorithms. More broadly, they had refined, assembled, and organized much of the best of what had been known and thought in computing, both the work of others and Knuth's own discoveries. In the words of one admiring colleague, Knuth's unfinished multivolume work had "established computer programming as computer science."

The title of the book amounted to an assertion. In one of his essays, Knuth examines the meanings of "art" over time, and he concludes: "We have seen that computer programming is an art, because it applies accumulated knowledge to the world, because it requires skill and ingenuity, and especially because it produces objects of beauty." He asserts: "Some programs are elegant, some are exquisite, some are sparkling. My claim is that it is possible to write *grand* programs, *noble* programs, truly magnificent ones!" In a book called *Literate Programming*, he sets out to show how programs can be explicated by their makers, not just to clarify their aims and methods but to turn them into works of art. "Programmers who subconsciously view themselves as artists will enjoy what they do and do it better," he writes.

He had created many programs of his own. The largest and best known is called T$_E$X (the name is derived from Greek and pronounced "tech"), a suite of software for computerized typesetting that includes a program for creating fonts. It was the first system that enabled computers to control the layout of text typographically and to print with the quality of hot-metal typesetting. Unlike many of the typesetting systems that followed, it adroitly handled mathematical and scientific notation. It was accounted a marvel when it first appeared, and more than thirty years later, both the original and variations of the system were still in use. Knuth never patented or licensed it; he had made the source code free and available to all.

His first publication was a spoof, "The Potrzebie System of Weights and Measures," published in *Mad* magazine in 1957, when he was nineteen. He had been a prolific and versatile writer ever since. His *Collected Papers* alone now filled eight volumes. He had written books about mathematics and the Bible, also a collection of lectures and essays aimed at a general audience. In one of these, "God and Computer Science," he writes: "I think it's fair to say that many of today's large computer programs rank among the most complex intellectual achievements of all time. They're absolutely trivial by comparison with any of the works of God, but they're still somehow closer to those works than anything else we know." The point is unusual. Many have professed to see the hand of God in nature. But, as Knuth would have it, computer science is "an *unnatural* science," a human invention that nonetheless opens a new lens on many theological questions. In the same lecture, Knuth suggests that programmers are positioned to catch "at least a glimmer of extra insight into the nature of God," because programming often entails the creation of "a small universe."

The nature of the art had changed in the span of Knuth's career. Huge so-called libraries of software had accreted. Nowadays, many programmers worked without writing a great deal of original code, instead assembling code that others had written. But the world still needed some people to write what Knuth called "the innards of these magic black boxes." Knuth said that his role in life was to serve this small cadre: "Somebody has to nurture them."

These were his 2 percent. It had taken a machine to liberate their talents, indeed to liberate Knuth's. He was not ungrateful. He considered *The Art of Computer Programming* the essence of his life's work, and he had chosen to dedicate it not to a person, but as follows:

This series of books is affectionately dedicated to the Type 650 computer once installed at Case Institute of Technology, with whom I have spent many pleasant evenings.

2

In the English family's house on Perham Street, the kitchen had contained seven boxes of cereal and flavors of ice cream, but there were no knickknacks on tables and few decorations on the walls. Paul's father fixed everything himself. "That's good enough," he'd declare, and for the next several years there would be an unpainted patch on a wall or wires hanging from a ceiling. Paul's mother, meanwhile, fashioned coffee filters out of paper towels, having calculated the relative expense.

One day in 1981, however, the summer after Paul's junior year at Boston Latin, his mother came home with a brand-new thing, new from the store and still fairly new in the world—a personal computer, called a Commodore VIC-20. It cost $299.99, less than other personal computers but a fortune in his parents' household. Paul couldn't figure out just why his mother had spent the money. Maybe it was the scent of importance, spread by ads that claimed computers were great for helping kids with their homework. It might also have been the fact that Paul's oldest brother, Ed, was now making a very good living programming computers.

The arrival of the VIC-20 felt like Christmas morning to Paul. Five years before, he had found it easy to turn away from the dumb terminals in the Latin School's basement, but this was an actual computer. Just taking the VIC-20 out of the box—it looked like a typewriter with some additional and mysterious keys—felt like an utterly different experience. The little machine didn't come with a display, but it was capable of producing images in color. Boston Gas had recently given Paul's father a new color TV for his years of loyal service. When his father wasn't home, Paul turned that TV, "the stupid box," into the VIC-20's screen. Hypothetically, the computer belonged to the entire household, but it was Paul who studied every one of the 164 pages of the VIC-20's manual. The machine came with a few games, which he and his siblings played until they were experts. When the others lost interest, Paul took sole possession.

The little house had a half-aboveground windowless basement, built as a garage but long since turned into a single bedroom. A cellar stairway led down from the kitchen. The room felt like a separate place, especially at night when everyone was up on the top floor, two stories above. The converted garage had served as a haven for male adolescence, the burrow of several teenage boys in turn, first for Ed and then for the next oldest, Tim, who remembered the room as the place where he could turn up his Led Zeppelin records and smoke pot in peace. When Tim left home, Paul inherited the place. He had long since given up selling drugs and he only rarely smoked marijuana, but he often felt as if he were taking a drug when he retreated to that dark, dank room and lay on the single bed with his earphones on, the sweet, sad songs of Joan Armatrading drowning out the gurgling of the water heater beside him. He carried the VIC-20 down there. He bought a secondhand color TV to serve as its monitor and taught himself to write small programs—in BASIC, the computer's built-in language. Later he would swear that the moment he saw computer code, he knew that he could write it. He could still get lost in lethargy down in his basement room, but much less often once the VIC-20 arrived.

During Paul's senior year at Latin, his brother Ed became a celebrity in the world of electronic games. Ed had left home and spent a year writing a chess-playing computer program for a company in Florida. It was a hit, and Parker Brothers had brought him back to New England and given him the task of converting a Japanese arcade game called Frogger into one that could be played at home on the Atari 2600 video game console. A difficult assignment, first of all because Atari didn't want other companies producing games for its device, which meant that Ed, with the help of a colleague, had to reverse-engineer the Atari console to figure out exactly how it worked. More daunting, Ed had to reproduce Frogger in a program that would occupy only a smidgen of memory. He pulled it off in just six weeks. His version of Frogger was the first electronic game accompanied by two-part-harmony music. He called the experience "an Olympic trial for game-making" and the finished product "my Mona Lisa."

Parker Brothers priced Ed's version of the game at $20 per cassette and was already shipping four million copies to retailers when Ed brought a cassette over to Perham Street to show his masterpiece to the family. He set up the equipment on the kitchen table, and everything was going well until Paul started fiddling with the controls. The next thing Ed knew, the game went haywire. What's more, Paul was able to make it malfunction again and again. Here was Ed's baby brother, whom Ed had known only distantly and mainly from contentious games of chess—which Ed, to his chagrin, had usually lost—

and now this teenage version of that irritating prodigy had found a bug in Ed's Mona Lisa. Ed was furious—"I coulda killed him!"—and then he was scared. The code for the game was contained in ROM, read-only-memory chips, which could not be reprogrammed. For some time, Ed waited to hear that others had found the bug and were returning their cassettes, but no one ever did. Parker Brothers, having sold all four million of those cassettes in a year, offered to pay Ed $50,000 for every game he programmed thereafter. Instead, Ed quit and started his own gaming company, and soon afterward bought a brand-new Porsche and a house on the waterfront south of Boston.

Paul was nineteen. Down in the converted garage, he began to code his own electronic game, on the VIC-20 and from scratch. He called the game Cupid. When he was done, it worked this way: The code drew a green field on the computer screen, then populated the field with five pink hearts, a green "ugly pill," and a circular face that represented Cupid, the player's alter ego. You moved Cupid around with a joystick, gobbling up the pink hearts while avoiding the arrows that shot across the screen horizontally and vertically. You, Cupid, could get killed by those arrows. You could also get blocked by them. Arrows that missed you would form latticed fences, hemming you in. But if you got Cupid positioned on top of an ugly pill, you turned green and also rubbery, and for a time you could squeeze through the fences of arrows. When you squeezed through, the program would make the computer produce a sound like the popping of a champagne cork. Paul spent a lot of time on the sound effects and on trying to code the behavior of pieces so they seemed like analogs of natural movements. Coding the sounds and the graphics was the kind of job programmers call "nontrivial," and it was equally hard to synchronize them.

Programming had come a long way by the time Paul made his

game. Computers are created with the built-in power to execute certain basic instructions, such as commands to add and subtract, and to perform operations that direct the flow of a program. These instructions are conveyed to the computer as discrete packages of high and low voltages, represented in what is called "machine language," a code that amounts to long skeins of zeros and ones. It is extraordinarily difficult to write programs in machine language. In the 1950s, not long after the creation of the first automatic digital computers, a system of symbols, another sort of code, was developed to represent those packages of zeros and ones. This system was called assembly language. It was easier to write than machine code but cumbersome at best.

The great step forward in programming came in the 1960s with the development of "high-level" languages. To give some sense of their power, imagine that Paul had been trying to create the standard beginner's program and tell his VIC-20 to print "Hello, World." Here is an example (produced by a program called the GNU C compiler) of what a part of a Hello, World program would have looked like, if Paul had written it in assembly language:

```
.file      "hello.c"
           .section    .rodata
.LC0:
           .string     "hello, world\n"
           .text
           .globl      main
           .type       main, @function
main:
.LFB0:
           .cfi_startproc
```

```
        pushl        %ebp
        .cfi_def_cfa_offset 8
        .cfi_offset 5, -8
        movl         %esp, %ebp
        .cfi_def_cfa_register 5
        andl         $-16, %esp
        subl         $16, %esp
        movl         $.LC0, (%esp)
        call         printf
        leave
        .cfi_restore 5
        .cfi_def_cfa 4, 4
        ret
        .cfi_endproc
.LFE0:
        .size        main, .-main
        .ident       "GCC: (GNU) 4.8.3"
        .section     .note.GNU-stack,"",@progbits
```

And here, by contrast, is the entire "Hello, World" program that Paul could have written in the early 1980s, using the VIC-20's built-in high-level language BASIC:

```
10 PRINT "Hello World!"
```

High-level languages allowed a coder to do vastly more in fewer lines of code. Fewer lines of code also made for fewer bugs in programs, and this too was significant. The gigantic programs soon to come could never have been written in assembly language. And they could never have been debugged well enough to be usable.

Paul's brother Ed was obliged to code Frogger in assembly language. So when Paul coded Cupid, he had it easier than Ed. But BASIC was an early and rather rudimentary high-level language, not easily bent to creating complex things such as sound effects. And like Ed with Frogger, Paul had to cram a great deal of functionality into a very small space. Ed had coded his Mona Lisa with only 4 kilobytes' worth of read-only memory chips. Paul, too, had to fit the Cupid program into 4 kilobytes of computer memory—and he had that much only because he found a way to borrow 500 bytes from the VIC-20's preloaded programs. These were small numbers even then, and minuscule a few decades later, when a smartphone that cost about as much as a VIC-20 contained memory circuits that could hold sixteen million times more data.

Donald Knuth writes: "One rather curious thing I've noticed about aesthetic satisfaction is that our pleasure is significantly enhanced when we accomplish something with limited tools." This was one source of the pleasure Paul felt when he finished Cupid. Indeed, he loved the whole procedure of creating programs. You write the code that should create a sound effect, you load it into the machine, and it doesn't work. So you study your code, you find the flaw in it, you run it again, and you keep on repeating the process until the machine does what you want. All the while you've been wrestling with the size of that code, striving to make it small enough to fit the computer's memory. You find ways to shorten it, and when at last it's concise enough and runs perfectly, you feel as if you've done something more than re-create the popping of a champagne cork.

Ed was astonished when Paul demonstrated the game for him. Engineers are known for frankness, a tendency that in Ed's case overcame sibling rivalry. "Wow!" he said. Then he told Paul, "Listen, there are companies paying real money for this stuff." With Ed's help, Paul sold Cupid to a company called Games by Apollo for $25,000. The company made a down payment of $5,000, then went out of business, but Paul wasn't very disappointed. He retrieved the rights to his game and used the $5,000 advance to buy a new Apple II personal computer, a printer, a floppy disk drive, and a "ROM oven"— a device for burning programs into integrated circuits, which he first used to make copies of Cupid for friends. He also bought a modem and talked his parents into paying for a second phone line, which he connected to his new modem in his basement bedroom.

The Internet was young. You had to search out correspondents. He went to one of the first meetings of the Boston Computer Society, where other enthusiasts handed out the phone numbers to their modems, and then he went home to his room and figured out how to write the code to connect his new computer to theirs. Modems worked slowly, which gave human eyes time to see how astonishing the process was. He would watch the files he was sending disappear gradually from his screen, and watch incoming files materialize bit by bit, as if they were being painted on an electronic canvas.

He was witnessing amazing things and also making them happen. Now and then he would hear sounds of the life of the house. The pipes to the water heater would start thumping, or there would be footsteps in the kitchen overhead. Upstairs, all the emotions of a big family were swirling around—arguments, many competing sorrows—and there was nothing he could do up there to change what worried and upset him. But he could always figure out how to tell the computer to do what he wanted, and it didn't argue back or ignore him. In his dark basement room, it could be any time of day or night, and when he was coding or watching a message being painted on his screen, he felt as though there was no other time than now and no other place but the small universe he was creating in his current program, a place where he was in charge, a refuge inside a refuge.

"I lived in my mind as a kid," Paul once said. He was still a small child when he began, on occasion, to see strange and wonderful apparitions in his bedroom. They usually appeared when he was just waking up. He would look at the clock on the face of his radio and it would have grown gigantic, and the outlet in the wall across the room would be six feet tall. He'd try to keep the wall socket just as big as a door, the clock as big as the moon, until eventually they shrank to their usual boring sizes. He didn't tell his parents about this. It wasn't exactly his secret. For a long time he assumed it wasn't worth mentioning, because it must be something everyone experienced.

There was reason to be quiet in his household. For Paul's first ten years, his mother was sick. She suffered from myasthenia gravis, an autoimmune disease that causes muscle weakness, sometimes in the muscles used in breathing. It is debilitating but only rarely fatal, and it wasn't as though she was sick all the time, but in bed at night Paul saw images of a wheelchair in the living room, an ambulance outside, a priest at the front door carrying his kit of sacred oil. So at those times when his father told the children they were going to kill their mother if they didn't quiet down, Paul knew that it was true.

His father's rules, as Paul understood them, were simple: no noise in the house and no motorcycle riding. He tried to be a good boy at home. School was another matter. When he arrived at first grade at St. Theresa's, he felt a certain freedom: "Inside my house it's strict. Outside my house I can do what I want." He liked to play little tricks on his young teacher. She often gave the class written quizzes. Paul would rush through them, getting all the answers right. She would still be handing out copies of the quiz when he finished his. Then he'd run up to her desk and smack his paper down beside her blotter. That poor young thing quit teaching after a year of him, Paul's mother said. He didn't believe it, but it might have been true.

At the end of that school year, according to family lore, the head nun at St. Theresa's told his mother, "Paul is a very special child. We believe he belongs at another school." In the seven years between nursery school and Boston Latin, Paul changed schools seven times. For some of those years he was placed in classes for the gifted and talented, but even then he usually felt cooped up and bored, and wherever he went he served time in detention.

When he was ten years old, his mother went to a Catholic priest who was said to have the power to heal those with great faith. She recovered and was never sick again. Of course, some feelings from that time remained with Paul. Some he carried through childhood in recurring memories: the times of stony silence between his parents, for example. After one tense morning, he was walking his little sister down Perham Street to school. She was crying. He was holding her hand, and he was crying, too, and ashamed of it because he was supposed to be her protector.

One memorable evening, Paul was sitting in the living room, watching his father watch TV, when someone outside started banging on the front door. His father opened it onto a tall, beefy, snarling man. "Your son beat the shit out of my son!" Paul's father was about six feet tall but wiry thin, much smaller than the man in the doorway. And yet, without any hesitation, Paul's father poked a finger in the man's chest and said, "Don't you *ever* bang on my door again!" And instantly, the big angry guy got quiet. He actually apologized. How did his dad do that? It seemed as if his dad had access to a magical power, like the power possessed by the good guys, the Jedis, in the *Star Wars* movies.

Once restored to health, Paul's mother was unquestionably in charge of the household. She cooked all the meals and served them at hours she appointed, and she never asked her husband for help in the kitchen or with the laundry or the cleaning, nor did he offer any. But she had never played the submissive housewife beloved by advertisers of the 1950s and '60s. She had gone to college, while Paul and his siblings suspected that their father had never finished high school. After her cure, Paul's mother became increasingly independent. "She decided to live again," Paul's brother Tim remembered, adding that it was also the mid-1970s, "the era when women were stepping out." She started playing tennis. She worked as a volunteer docent at the Boston Public Library and the Arnold Arboretum, adjacent to West Roxbury. She began to study the family genealogy as a hobby. She also worked as a substitute teacher, and one day, to everyone's surprise, she announced that she was going to buy her own car.

Paul's father argued with her. They had a family car, an old Plymouth Grand Fury, which she could use whenever she wanted.

She said, "I'm getting my own car."

She chose a standard shift, not an automatic, and most astonishing of all, she chose a Honda—"a damned foreign car," Paul's father said.

She knew a lot about a lot of things, such as birds and botany and classical music. She was the one who insisted on buying a piano for the house and who arranged music lessons for the younger children, lessons that Paul, alone among his siblings, relished. In Paul's baby book, his mother wrote of him at three years old: "Doesn't ride trike much now, but has constant interest in trucks & cars. Always busy & never bored. Very friendly child. Seldom indoors—plays with anyone. Amazing conversationalist. We love to hear him talk—tells us stories. Great imagination. Wants to grow 'bigger' so he can touch the sky. Wants to be superman & runs around with towel-cape." Clearly, she felt affection for him, but even after her cure, he never felt great warmth from her. Maybe there were just too many children and not enough of her to go around.

In any case, it was mainly his father to whom Paul looked for guidance. His father could be gruff, and sometimes Paul imagined anger radiating from him, along with the sweet smell from the cocktail glass on the table by the easy chair. But his father wasn't a drunk and wasn't usually angry, and when he was, Paul would try, even as a schoolboy, to imagine what it must be like to work all day and come home to seven noisy kids and a sick wife. And his dad had a shiny side. He was a prankster and a great storyteller, especially at the dinner table. There was this guy at Boston Gas who boasted endlessly about the good mileage he got from his Volkswagen. If he had served in World War II in Europe, as Paul's father had, he would never have bought a *German* car. How to stop the guy's boasting? Well, Paul's father said, every day for about a week he sneaked out to the parking lot and poured gas into the VW's fuel tank, and then when the guy began telling everyone that his car's great mileage was *actually increasing,* Paul's father started siphoning gas out of the fuel tank. And then, just to top things off, he and some other men from work sneaked over to the fellow's house one night, lifted the Volkswagen over his fence, and left it sitting in his front yard.

Paul's father was a second-generation Irish American, son of a woman who had come from Ireland as a teenager. For a time she had worked as a servant for a lace-curtain Irish family who insisted that she walk several paces behind them when they went to church in their finery. Paul's father was only eighteen when his own father died, and to support his mother and five sisters he had gone to work as an apprentice pipe fitter for Boston Gas. No one without a college degree, Paul gathered, had ever risen as high in that company as his father. Once when Paul was still in grade school, his father took him to lunch with some other midlevel executives. Paul felt shy in the company of those strangers, and it worried him when his father ordered first one Manhattan and then another. It seemed like a lot to drink at lunch, but the other men had drinks, too, and it was clear that his dad was someone they looked up to, from the way they bent forward when he talked, from the hearty way they laughed at his jokes. Paul wished he could be like that, sure of himself, the life of the party.

On weekends and evenings, his father always seemed to have a do-it-yourself project, and Paul and his next-older brother, Danny, were usually eager to help, starting from the time when they were still very young and their father praised them for being good at holding flashlights while he worked on the furnace. Soon he was teaching them how to sweat pipes and snake wires behind walls and fix carburetors. He helped them build a clubhouse behind the garage.

Paul's father also made a small side business out of buying, repairing, and selling used appliances. It made sense that a man with seven kids would look to make some extra money, but Paul soon realized that this business was mostly a game his father played, for the sake of the hunt and the sport of bargaining. His father would check the paper for announcements of dates when the wealthy nearby towns of Newton and Brookline were going to pick up residents' discarded appliances. He'd head for those suburbs on the evenings before the scheduled pickups, bringing one or two of his older sons to help him with the heavy lifting. When he found a fairly new washing machine sitting at the curb, he and his boys would load it into the old family station wagon. He'd take the machine to Perham Street and fix it. "Nine times out of ten there's just a piece of underwear wrapped around the spinner," he'd say. Once he had the machine repaired, he'd put it up for sale in one of the local papers or in *The Want Advertiser*, which he also studied regularly, looking for used cars and appliances to buy.

By the time Paul became a regular on the buying trips, his dad was mainly dealing in window-mounted air conditioners, much easier for a man with an aging back to lift and put in the car. His dad's general scheme was to buy the ACs in late fall or winter, repair them when he had the time, and wait until the hot days of summer to sell them. He made many of his purchases at yard sales. Paul studied his techniques. Say his dad liked the looks of an air-conditioning unit on sale for a hundred dollars. He'd go up to the owner, and he'd start by cracking a joke. Maybe the seller would say, by way of claiming that the AC unit in question was virtually brand-new, "I bought it for my aunt, and she passed away." Paul's dad would smile. "Well, she probably needs air-conditioning where she is now."

Paul imagined the other party thinking *Who is this guy?* His dad was trying to catch the seller off guard, Paul thought. Then right away, his dad would name a price, always a crazy number: "I'll give you three dollars for that piece of junk." And surprisingly often the seller would say, "Oh. I guess." To Paul it seemed as if, having been thrown off balance, the seller needed something tangible, like a number, to get steadied.

Sometimes his dad would walk near a seller sitting in a lawn chair and catch the seller's eye and hold it. But he'd keep on walking, and, as if it were an afterthought, he'd flick his thumb toward the air conditioner in question, saying, "I'll give you five bucks for that." He would use other sorts of movement to mesmerize his adversaries— a snap of the fingers, a shifting of the shoulders, a cocking of the head, which tended to make people lean toward him. He would also lower his voice and use long pauses to achieve the same effect. Above all, his dad would make himself a picture of confidence. That was the central rule of negotiating, he told Paul: You had to be confident in order to look confident, and that meant you had to be prepared to walk away from something you really wanted if you couldn't get your terms. And if you never walked away, you weren't negotiating hard enough.

———————

Paul was mindful of his father's sayings on every subject, but the one that haunted him—"You're all the same"—made him feel he had to make a separate life away from home. He didn't expect or receive much recognition for his accomplishments: first place in an MIT-sponsored chess championship for youngsters when he was in fourth grade, first place in the Boston Science Fair when he was in sixth, fourth place in the National Toy Design Award Competition in eighth. His parents didn't come to watch when the Latin School played for the soccer championship of Boston, even though Paul was on the team, or to the concerts at Symphony Hall and the Hatch Shell on the Esplanade, where Paul played his trumpet in the Latin School's jazz band. Paul forgave them. His parents couldn't possibly have gone to all their seven children's games and concerts, and maybe they felt that if they couldn't go to one child's performances, they shouldn't go to any. He thought of himself as flourishing in secret. The sheer size of his family made this easy to pull off, and it also often left him free to do much as he pleased, to roam the streets and subway tunnels of Boston during the school years and to play at what used to be called juvenile delinquency during the summer.

When Paul was a baby, his parents bought a ramshackle cottage— for $5,200—on Helen Street in the seaside town of Hull, a half hour's drive from Boston. Every June the family packed up and moved there. His mother brought the toaster from Perham Street—no sense in wasting money on two toasters. And his father brought his tools and worked on fixing up their cottage in his usual that's-good-enough spirit. Hull was a town in a pretty setting, but it wasn't fancy like some other towns in the area—like Cohasset, where kids rode around in their daddies' Porsches, Paul and his friends would tell each other. Hull had a yacht club. "But," Paul would say, "they only drink Budweiser there." The town had some public housing apartment buildings as well as seaside cottages, and it contained Nantasket Beach, huge and public and thronged with kids and, by the end of summer days, covered with litter. "Trashbasket Beach," he and his summer friends called it.

Paul and Danny reveled in that town, often in the company of three other boys: "the Hull Five." Paul and Danny got a pirate flag and painted the gang's name on it, then they broke into the high school and raised the flag on its roof. They found a styrofoam mannequin's head and torso and adorned it with a blouse borrowed from one of their sisters, and a wig and glow-in-the-dark eyes and lipstick. They mounted the figure on a broomstick and carried it around their neighborhood at night, tapping it against second-story windowpanes so that the people who looked out would see a woman floating in the dark.

Driver's licenses opened up a whole new theater of operations. Paul installed a good stereo in one of his cars. In the very early morning hours, he and his buddies would drive the car to Trashbasket Beach, leave it in the best parking spot, then go home to bed. They'd return on their bikes once the crowds began to gather, and Paul would get his speakers out of the trunk, connect them to his car's stereo, set them up on the sidewalk, turn on the music, and wait—it rarely failed—for girls to arrive in their bikinis.

Together, he and Danny created a remote-control system so they could shoot bottle rockets from under the rear end of Danny's Camaro, sometimes at tailgating cars. Meanwhile, Paul began accumulating speeding tickets, often while driving his own secondhand and lovingly restored Camaro on the circuitous route from West Roxbury to Hull. He totaled two cars while in high school, one of them when he ran into a school bus on the Jamaicaway.

Paul, it seems, was capable in his youth of two very different kinds of behavior. In the abstract, this is not strange; teenagers are often contradictory beings. But it is hard to reconcile the images Paul drew of himself, of a boy often lost in ferocious anger, and the boy in a photograph from junior year in high school—thin and tall and gentle-looking, indeed almost feminine.

Serious fighting began for him in fifth grade. This was also around the time when the federal court began its attempt to integrate Boston's public schools—by busing African American children into white working-class sections of the city. West Roxbury could not have been less integrated. In the census, the entire town was listed as 100 percent "white." Paul found himself in homeroom with a tall and burly black-skinned boy, a new kind of person. The kid's mere presence frightened Paul, and this meant he had to pick a fight with him. Paul fought him to a bloody draw in a school hallway, and they ended up in detention together, where Paul discovered that the guy was funny. They became friends, and through him Paul met one of his cousins, who was herself a cousin of Donna Summer's. Paul didn't get to meet her, but it was exciting to come that close to a famous singer.

By high school his fights had assumed a pattern. A friend and sometimes even a stranger who was small or weak or in some way vulnerable would be getting picked on by a tough kid, and at once Paul would feel hand-shaking fury, as if he were the one being bullied. He would rush to intervene. There was the kid, later jailed for attempted murder, who went after a friend of Paul's on Dent Street, a block over from Perham. He and Paul faced off, pushing each other in the chest, and then Paul put his foot behind the tough kid's foot and shoved him backward, tripping him. Then he jumped on him and started punching. There was the time at the gym when another tough kid, a very big kid, was trying to take a ball away from a friend of his, and Paul got in between them and said, "Hey, fuck off," and the kid squared himself up, and Paul, thinking *I have one shot*, punched him in the jaw as hard as he could. The kid fell and started crying. "My big brother's gonna beat you up," he wailed.

"Dude, *you* could beat me up," said Paul, standing over him. "Why do you need your big brother?"

Paul thought of this as bullying bullies. He was playing the vigilante. But he couldn't account for his most terrible fight. A smartass kid at the bus stop. Paul banged the boy's head on the sidewalk. When sanity returned, Paul got up and backed away. To his relief, the kid got up and ran. For days afterward, the scene kept returning, and Paul would think *I could have killed him. God, I could have* killed *him.*

Two of his brothers knew about some of his fights, but even best friends from high school were astonished when, years later, Paul recounted his days of brawling. One former girlfriend said the news distressed her: "That was not the person I knew. I thought he was the smartest boy in the whole world. I thought he was the *sweetest* boy in the whole world." She remembered him as confident, even a bit competitive, traits she found attractive. He wasn't content, as she was, to be just a cashier at the local drugstore, he had to be the head cashier. And yet he was kind to everyone under him, especially to her, always making sure at the end of their shift that her drawer contained just the right amount of cash. She was both "shocked" and "dismayed," she said, when she ran into him years later and he told her that he often went to nightclubs nowadays. When he was her boyfriend, he was shy and serious. His idea of a fun date was to sit in the '68 Camaro that he'd rebuilt and customized, and wait for people to come by and say, "Hey, nice ride." She said, "He really liked that. I thought it was neat." But she also liked to dance and sing, and he never wanted to go out on the town, which was one reason they broke up. "I cried in my room all weekend," she said.

A high school girlfriend who used to go to Mass with Paul remembered his taking her on dates to the Boston Public Library, where he would help her with her homework. He carved their initials in trees and in the snow, and one time he artfully printed them, via his computer, on a huge piece of paper, the first letters of their names drawn with tiny versions of the same letters.

She thought he was the perfect boyfriend, and her mother thought so, too. Unlike Paul's parents, hers came to see him play in the jazz band at the Hatch Shell. One time she told him she wanted a phone in her room, and he said, "I can do that," and then came to her house and hooked up an extension. She smiled at the memory. "Then we could talk for hours." She remembered being very impressed when he showed her his video game, and she swore she would always remember his telling her, "I like the way you think." She called this "the best compliment I ever got in my life." Decades later, she read Paul's own account of fighting and drug dealing as a teenager—in an interview published in a magazine called *Entrepreneur*. She preferred her version of him. "He was sweet and gentle. I never knew him to fight, smoke pot, or even swear! And over thirty years later, that is how I will always remember him (no matter what he says!)."

Paul was a boy who, feeling shy, made himself gregarious, who always had plenty of friends and was never long without a girlfriend, who loved being on a team and especially in a band, who worried when he sensed anger in the house and wished that he could cure it, who was often in ardent pursuit of "fun" and was devoted to breaking rules and yet was rarely without a job, and was so conscientious that one time, feeling too ill to drive after a night on the town with some buddies, he took a taxi to his post as head Medi-Mart cashier. The taxi cost him more than his entire day's pay, and his father scolded him for the extravagance.

In later years, Paul and all his siblings compared their memories of family life in the presence of a psychologist. Afterward, Paul concluded, "There are seven different versions of our childhood, all of them true." Some versions were sunny. The one most nearly like Paul's came from his older brother Tim, who remembered weddings that their whole family had attended, all of the English boys and girls sitting silently at a table while members of other families danced and socialized. Tim imagined people whispering, "Look at those English kids." At seven, Tim had become convinced that theirs was the weirdest family on the block. "You didn't talk about family business outside, or for that matter *within* the family."

But these were the feelings of one who had fled—Tim set out on his bicycle for California and never returned for good. Paul was still in high school then, and the departures of older siblings were mournful events. He felt the age-old sadness, the feeling that he was being left behind and that the family was crumbling. Paul had just started high school when Ed left for the chess-programming job in Florida. *Why is he doing this?* Paul had thought. Then Tim left, and then his oldest sister, Eileen. Paul had never felt especially close to those three, they were so much older. He began writing to Eileen, however. He sent her detailed instructions about writing to another sister who was going to a local college. He told Eileen to compliment a sister who had joined Weight Watchers: "When you write to us next (YOU BETTER WRITE SOON AND A LONG LETTER) say, 'Oh my gosh, you look skinny!'" He closed the letters, "Love always, your little brother Paul."

In one letter, he described an evening he was spending with their father in the house on Perham Street. "It's 11:45 pm and me & Dad are having a stubborn contest to see who will go upstairs first. He's being absorbed by the stupid box as usual. Its his own new color one he got from BGC for his 40 yrs. We've been sitting here for an hour. As soon as I go upstairs though he will go up and knock on the bathroom door." A page later Paul added, "Dad keeps half snoring & then yawning. That last snore did it. I quit! You win Dad! I can't take it! I'm going to bed! Arrrrggghhhh!" Not the most flattering portrait of his dad, but this was a Friday night when Paul always had fun things to do, and he had chosen to spend it with his father.

3

In tenth grade at Boston Latin, Paul had received career counseling and had been told he should become a priest, a therapist, or an actuary. "What's an actuary?" he had wondered. College counseling was offered in eleventh grade, but he had skipped it. He didn't care about college. He was going to become a professional musician.

Twenty-six of his fellow students got into Harvard. Paul graduated near the bottom of his class and didn't apply to Harvard or anywhere else. By the time his mother learned that his SAT scores entitled him to free tuition at the state's schools, all the deadlines had passed except the one at the Boston branch of the University of Massachusetts. She insisted that Paul visit. He enrolled, but only because he learned that the school had a student jazz band. The campus was situated on the seashore, on Columbia Point, facing Dorchester Bay. Its monolithic buildings, only eight years old, didn't live up to the setting. Fellow students called the campus "the prison" and "the fortress." It was a commuter school, in prestige not far above a community college.

In his first days there, Paul often found himself sitting at the back of classrooms, imagining old classmates surrounded by the grand-looking buildings of Harvard Yard. *And I'm at UMass Boston,* he would think. He thought of his old friend Mike from Hull, now at Boston College, another first-rate school. He'd had the same chances as Mike and the others, and he'd blown them. He was just a screwup, at a school that looked like it was built for screw-ups.

One day early in the first semester, Paul was sitting gloomily in a social sciences class when the instructor invited the students to debate the morality of the Vietnam War. Within moments, the room came alive for Paul. The man to his right, it turned out, was sitting in a wheelchair because of wounds from Vietnam. The older man in the chair to Paul's left had lost a son to the war. Listening to them felt like a lesson not just about history but also about social class— about his own people, the class of Americans who had done most of the fighting in Vietnam. *My friend Mike is not having this experience,* he thought. *He's with kids in polo shirts over at BC.*

A door had opened for Paul. A humble place like UMass Boston had its own virtues, once you really let yourself in. There were many night classes, which meant Paul could work his way through college, as many other students had to do. There was also the jazz band and the chance to learn about other cultures, and not just from books but in person.

One evening, Paul was walking down a windowless, fluorescent-lit hallway in one of the buildings of the fortress when he heard an odd concatenation of sounds—quick, sharp slaps of wood on wood and loud exclamations in an Asian language. He stopped at once, then followed the sounds into the student lounge, where two young men were playing what looked for a moment like chess. But the pieces weren't the standard figurines of chess. They were identical wooden disks differentiated only by Chinese characters painted on their flat round tops. The young men played fast, slapping their pieces down on each other's pieces, then slapping those captured pieces onto the table beside the board with exclamations that seemed to put those noises into words. The whole thing seemed more tactile than chess, athletic as well as cerebral. Paul thought, *I have to learn how to play that.*

Paul made friends with the students. Both were Vietnamese, and the game, they told Paul, was called xiangqi—pronounced approximately *shung-chee*. Its origins are obscure. It might be several hundred years old or a thousand, and had long been the most widely played board game in China, which meant it was almost certainly the most widely played game in the world. It was also popular in Vietnam, where one of the young men had earned a sort of living as a xiangqi hustler. The other student was named Trung Dung. One time Paul took him out to lunch in his Camaro, and he had to show Trung how to put on a seatbelt. For his part, Trung taught Paul how to play xiangqi and beat him at it relentlessly over the next several years. Paul stuck with it regardless. He read books about the game. He searched for opponents, carrying his own xiangqi set to places like the Asian student lounge at MIT. He spent much of his scant free time in Chinatown, watching the old men play.

UMass proved to be the place where Paul found his vocation. He had arrived there still believing he would become a musician. He had no other plan. He had been working part-time for his brother Ed's new company, coding music and sound effects into video games. But he thought of programming as a hobby, not as the sort of thing one studied in college, let alone as part of a science. When he saw a listing for a class called "Introduction to Computer Science Using Pascal," he thought he might as well check it out. It was a lecture course, with about a hundred students in a big windowless room. After a few preliminary classes, the professor started assigning homework, and by then Paul felt in the mood for doing some. In one of the first assignments, Paul had to write a procedure, an algorithm, that would make a computer sort a list of numbers in reverse order. Sorting was a classic problem with myriad applications. It had been solved in many elegant ways over the brief history of computing, but all the members of the class, including the instructor, were supposed to invent their own solutions. At the next session, the instructor unveiled his code, writing it out boldly on the board. Peering from his seat far back in the room, Paul saw that his own algorithm was shorter than the professor's. It would do the job faster, he thought. He was surprised, and he was pleased. *I'm way smarter than this guy,* he thought. And then he thought, *I could do pretty well at this stuff.*

One by one Paul's older brothers and sisters moved away from home, but Paul stayed on in the converted garage for all the seven years he studied at the university. He had enough money to rent his own place, and he certainly wasn't lazy. He had spent part of the summer before college as a meter reader for Boston Gas. He loved the job, perhaps too much. On one of his first days, he read eight hundred meters. In union parlance, he did "two books," and the union boss took him aside and said, "From now on, you'll do one book." After a while, he was put on "special reads," which meant he had to find his way inside places where the meters hadn't been read in six months. Sometimes he had to break in. The job had excitements. It was always possible that he would find someone inside with a gun. It was fascinating, too, like a tour of the innards of the city, all sides of it, from townhouses on Beacon Hill furnished in mahogany to restaurant basements in Chinatown and Southie haunted by enormous rats.

He left that job reluctantly. He went on coding part-time for his brother during most of freshman year while also playing in the jazz band. He loved the teamwork, the call and response of playing in a band, and especially the complex task of arranging music, which felt akin to the programming he was doing in his classes, indeed much more like computer programming than math had ever seemed.

He took most of his classes at night, and as many in computer science as he was allowed. During the days, he worked full-time, at a string of programming jobs seven years long. Soon enough he realized that, in spite of first impressions, the computer science faculty at lowly UMass Boston deserved his respect. Some were still in the midst of distinguished careers, and most had practical experience at companies. Unlike many computer science programs, theirs focused not on theory but on the actual engineering of software. Paul's jobs added up to a supplemental course, like clinical rotations in medical school.

It was the 1980s, and computer technologies were still a source of wonder and anxiety to the American public, but they no longer belonged exclusively to specialists in white coats ministering to huge mainframe machines in sealed-off rooms. The invention of the microchip—the innards of a computer etched onto tiny slices of silicon—had made possible a great variety of machines and uses for them. Other devices had all but replaced centralized computer systems like the one Paul had broken into at Boston Latin. There were supercomputers, minicomputers, workstations, and personal computers, and all that machinery required the services of software engineers. During the 1980s, their numbers grew annually by more than 25 percent. Computers were spreading even into the humble corners of American life, into car repair shops and living rooms and grade schools, as well as into labs and government buildings and corporate skyscrapers. The computer had—all of a sudden, it seemed—become America's essential tool, favorite new toy, and universal scapegoat. Everywhere in the land, one now heard the phrase "Sorry, the computer's down."

To many parents of kids in junior high and elders in business and education, it seemed as if the new technologies had arrived with a human user interface included, with a generation genetically coded to understand how computers worked. In his first programming job, Paul was hired as a temp doing menial chores, but ended up rewriting the company's administrative software. He had wanted to learn what office work was like. After about six months, he quit and signed on at a medical device company, where he wrote a program to control a centrifuge. He also spent a year and a half with a defense contractor, writing software to control a high-speed camera in an air force spy plane and a user manual to go with it; and another year and a half at the minicomputer company Data General, where he performed coding jobs for a team of computer scientists with PhDs.

In 1987, Paul finished that practicum, and he also got his bachelor's degree. He was twenty-four and ready, he felt, for bigger things. His favorite professor at UMass was a computer scientist with a doctorate named Bob Morris. He worked part-time for a large and growing company called Interleaf. It made software for the computerized creation of documents, and it had within its ranks, Paul gathered, a small group of extraordinary programmers. Paul asked Morris if he could join them. Morris said Paul wasn't ready yet. "All right, whatever," said Paul, and he went to work for one of Interleaf's small competitors. Like the great majority of the fourteen thousand software companies founded in the 1980s, this one was doomed to roughly the same life span as a salmon's, but it lasted long enough for Paul to learn some of the new art behind electronic publishing. Meanwhile, he went on studying at UMass. The PhDs he had met at Data General inspired him. He wanted an advanced degree, too.

By the time he started graduate classes, Paul knew his way around the society of programmers. He felt he was one of them, and yet he sometimes felt like an anthropologist in their midst. He knew coders so unworldly that they needed a mnemonic to guide them at a restaurant table. They'd murmur "BMW" to remind themselves that it was their Bread that lay on the small plate to the left of their Meal, their Water in the glass to the right. He could navigate the wider world better than many programmers, and he felt comfortable among them. He felt that all of them were a bit peculiar: "We're all introverts, we're all nerds, we're all slightly awkward." And he could more than hold his own technically, which was what really mattered in the society of coders.

At UMass Boston, Computer Science consisted mainly of two rooms, aboveground but subterranean in feeling, a little windowless world of concrete floors and concrete-block walls painted industrial white. There was a lab stuffed with equipment and next door a fairly large room filled with tables and chairs. This was where grad students hung out with computers and each other.

Paul's main friend there was a thin young man with long blond hair named Karl Berry. Paul could usually find him sitting in front of one of the new Sun-3 workstation computers. The machines were named "red," "blu," and "grn." In this society, abbreviation was a useful habit, and naming machines was one of the things that some coders thought of as "a fun event." Karl struck Paul at first as one of those programmers who had trouble looking other people in the eye, a difficulty that Paul had tried to overcome in himself. Karl had a deep, strong voice, though, and strong opinions. He could be curt and impatient when discussing technical matters, but he struck Paul as very smart and principled and, once you got to know him, downright friendly. Karl was also a very good programmer, one of the two or three best who hung out in that room. Maybe in another setting

Paul would have decided to make him a rival, but probably not. Paul never had the feeling that Karl wanted to compete with him. Karl felt more like a colleague, like a fellow member of a band that played the rarefied music of computer code. Karl was the first member of Paul's band, as it turned out, a charter member of his twenty-pluses.

They were nearly the same age. Both had their first encounter with computers in seventh grade, though Karl's early romance was more innocent and chaperoned. His family was living in Palo Alto for a year, one of the few places in the late 1970s where a junior high school student was apt to find a formal class in programming. Learning to code had felt immediately comfortable to Karl, as it had to Paul, like developing an inborn trait. You wrote the program just so, and in no time you saw the correct answer appear, an answer worked out not by you but by the machine under your command. This was powerful stuff, magical in the sense of Arthur C. Clarke's third law of prediction: "Any sufficiently advanced technology is indistinguishable from magic."

After Palo Alto, Karl's family had returned to Canton, in upstate New York, the home of St. Lawrence University, where his mother taught music. On holidays and college vacations, Karl would use a plastic card to jimmy open the door to the university's computer lab, where he spent hours reading manuals and trying out what he learned. What he later called the social niceties didn't come easily to him, but that didn't matter with computers. Exploring them didn't require that he deal with other people and their complexities. Writing software seemed to occupy a place between pure mathematics and the experimental sciences, between the search for a platonic ideal and the search for theories that jibed with observations of nature. He referred to writing software as "this funny business." It was the creation of something "notional/fictional/imaginary" that nonetheless had tangible effects. Coding was infinitely precise and yet imperfectible. Programs got written and revised until they did their jobs as well as possible. It was, Karl thought, a field for people who liked "the idea of good enough instead of perfect, the idea of play around in your head instead of play around in the mud." If your program failed, it was because you hadn't tried hard enough, not because information was withheld or missing. Programming computers felt, Karl would say, like entering "a universe unto itself."

He had been a model student in high school, especially compared to Paul, and went on to Dartmouth to study the almost brand-new field of computer science. One day in 1983, his professor handed him a tape that contained some new software, saying, "You're a bright guy, Karl. Go and install this stuff." The tape contained Donald Knuth's typesetting system TEX and the handbook Knuth had written for it, *The TEXbook*. It began: "GENTLE READER: This is a handbook about TEX, a new typesetting system intended for the creation of beautiful books—and especially for books that contain a lot of mathematics."

Karl loved it, the clarity of Knuth's prose style and the central idea behind the TEX software: that via a computer one could create art. And you could use TEX free of charge and change it however you wanted, so long as you didn't call your modified version TEX. This wasn't very unusual then. As Karl would put it, "Universities were still about sharing knowledge (instead of cashing in on it)." Karl would also say that he had his best luck socially through the computer. He had met his first girlfriend on one of the early online news and discussion groups. She was a typographer and a TEX enthusiast.

In the 1960s, IBM created a complex operating system called DOS and all but gave it away—to Microsoft, then a small company. In the years since, software had become an increasingly valuable commodity, and companies were turning the programs their employees wrote into private estates, surrounded by walls of secrecy, restrictive copyright licenses, and eventually patents. Meanwhile, a movement of programmers had begun to grow up in opposition. It ultimately became what amounted to a large, informal commune of great significance, which advanced the state of the art, kept the Internet and World Wide Web free for all to use, and produced those great libraries of code that anyone could borrow from, including entrepreneurs.

The progenitor of this movement was a legendary programmer named Richard Stallman. He founded something called the Free Software Foundation. Karl came across it in its early days, and was drawn to it at once. "Share and share alike": that was how Karl summed up the philosophy. He argued the case with Paul sometimes, down in the computer room.

"I won't invest a lot of R&D effort in my company if someone can just rip me off by copying all my ideas," Paul wrote in one email to Karl, arguing for limited software patent protection. In another, he wrote: "I don't like the idea of throwing out the baby with the bath water, killing software patents all together."

Karl replied that it would be far better to have no software patents at all than the thousands upon thousands of patents that claimed ownership of software that by rights, and even by statute, should have belonged to everyone. Many patents were so broad that they encompassed elements fundamental to programming, elements long in the public domain. And there were so many of those kinds of patents that programmers often had no way of knowing which ones they might be violating as they wrote their code.

The argument widened at times. Paul wrote, for instance: "Capitalism American-style says that a million people all acting selfishly and *without regard for others* somehow create something reasonable."

"I disagree that that is the case," replied Karl.

In Karl, Paul had met someone who stood for an ideal. Paul was an idealist, too, but also a pragmatist, and a lot less innocent than Karl. It would have been hard to imagine Karl dealing pot or shooting bottle rockets at tailgating cars. At one point Karl wrote, on the wisdom of abolishing software patents: "I hope I can convince you. If I can't convince you, I despair."

Paul hung out with Karl and his girlfriend—she was a fellow master's student—on many evenings in the main computer science room at UMass. To Karl, it seemed as though a lot of the other students there were learning this trade just to land jobs with good pay. He and Paul didn't talk about that sort of thing. They traded thoughts on the craft of programming and on their other enthusiasms, which they were combining with programming. Paul just then was very interested in writing synthesizers, code that could turn a computer into a musical instrument. Karl and his girlfriend were fascinated with typesetting and the grand suite of software that Knuth had created for digital typography.

At the end of the master's program, students were divided into teams of four or five, each team to work cooperatively on creating a substantial program. Paul and Karl and his girlfriend asked that they be placed on the same team, but the professor demurred. They were his best students, and he wanted them spread around. The course was supposed to teach a process. The product didn't really matter. But it wasn't very long before Paul went to the professor and told him that his teammates didn't know what they were doing. Why didn't he let Paul do the project by himself? He could do it in half the time the team would take. "You don't understand what this course is about," the professor answered. "*I* could do the project in half the time, but I'm not going to, and neither are you. What you *are* going to do is teach your team and get the project done on time." Paul complied, happily enough.

Afterward, he and Karl both stayed on in Boston, but they went separate ways. Karl and his girlfriend got jobs at the Free Software Foundation, where they went to work on creating a digital family of fonts, a very challenging task in that era. Paul went to his professor Bob Morris and asked him again if he could have a job at Interleaf. This time Morris said, "Okay. You're ready now."

4

BOSTON'S SOCIAL STRUCTURE HAD ACCRETED OVER FOUR CENTU-
ries. By tradition, certain routes to success were blocked for someone
like Paul. In one world, people pronounced "wheelbarrow" as if the
word were "wheelbarrel," and like Paul got married in a Polish Catholic church in Dorchester. And in the other, girls learned excellent
posture and grew up saying "toe-*mah*-toe," not "tamayta," and a lad
went to country day school, then prep school, and then, if his grades
were merely decent, Harvard, where he would be examined during
"punching season" and invited to join a final club—the invitation
guaranteed if it had been his father's club and he was a "legacy." A
family address in Louisburg Square, a brass plate on the door, a father who took you to Brooks Brothers or maybe his tailor to buy your
first suit. Money lay behind the whole construction, of course, but
when it came to membership, manners mattered more than money.
If you didn't have a trust fund awaiting you at twenty-one, and even if
your parents had fallen to shabby gentility, you could still land a job
at an institution like the State Street Bank and Trust, and work among

mahogany and the models of the sorts of sailing ships that had founded the old fortunes still being managed there. You'd be hired in the certainty that your boss could take you out to lunch at the Somerset Club and wouldn't have to ask the steward to outfit you with a proper jacket and tie. You would carry in your accent the assurance that you knew the difference between the fish fork and the salad fork, and of course you would never have to murmur "BMW."

One could feel excluded from that world even after being admitted to one of its favored institutions. In his autobiography, Tom White wrote about going to college in the 1930s: "I did not like attending Harvard—especially the first two years when I was a commuter. I had a poor self-image to start with and felt inferior to some of the good-looking, self-assured wealthy young guys. There was a separate house for commuters on a side street off Harvard Square. Commuters used it to study, have a meal or a snack, or just rest for a while. I even hated going in there. I just hated the fact that I was a townie I guess." In later life, Tom made the acquaintance of a scion of one of Boston's founding elite, Alexander Forbes. "Sandy was class of 1932 at Harvard, handsome guy, a real Brahmin, just like the Cabots and the Lowells, spoke only to God," Tom wrote. The last time Tom ran into Forbes, the man was pushing ninety. He said to Tom, "Things change as you go through life, and we don't feel about you people the way we used to." *You people.* By then, Tom wrote, he felt only amusement.

One can overstate the exclusionary power exercised by Boston's Anglo-Saxon elite. There had long been ways for a young Irish Catholic to rise. Tom had found one, in construction. "In my business," he liked to say, "all you had to be was low bidder." There was politics, of course. And thanks to recent economic history, there was another and broadening route up, the technological exception. You could have the wrong accent and no table manners, and be possessed by psychological oddities or worse, so long as you belonged among Knuth's 2 percent, born to program computers.

Enthusiasts imagined that digital technologies would serve as a great democratizing, equalizing force. At worst this was sheer fantasy, and at best just one of many distant possibilities in the kaleidoscope of the future. But there was one social revolution that computers certainly performed. Out on the highways that half encircled Boston—Route 128 and I-495—great clutters of new computer-related companies were arising. Most of the buildings had all the grace and style of grids on graph paper—quickly built, inexpensive, functional. The founder might be an immigrant's son with a knack for engineering, his office suite decked out in wallpaper that vaguely looked like wood paneling. Downstairs, in cubicles and windowless labs, engineers were producing stuff that was in turn producing immense new fortunes. For those in the business of making or selling it, computer technology really was a new way to rise. Merit counted more in the business of computer programming than in most professions. And for boys, at least, the road from software engineer to software entrepreneur, from wage earner to company founder, was already well marked out, there for the taking when Paul arrived at Interleaf in 1989.

———————

For Paul, 1989 was a year of formal steps to adulthood. He was twenty-five. He got married and bought a house—he chose one about the size of his family's house on Perham Street—and he started what he thought of as his first real job. The man who hired Paul at Interleaf was a business executive named Larry Bohn. He wasn't a programmer himself, but he was, as Paul would later say, a shrewd observer of programmers. Bohn gave Paul a low-level task for starters, and Paul made a face as if to say, "Are you kidding me? I could do that in my sleep." He did the job in no time and soon afterward was made a member of the product development group, or "prodvlp," also known, to some of its members anyway, as "the elite group." There were fewer than a dozen of them. Paul was the youngest.

The 1980s had been a time of ferment in the world that Paul was joining. Inventions in hardware and software routinely came out of places like Bell Labs, Xerox PARC, MIT, Stanford, Carnegie Mellon. Then others crowded around the new things, improving, refining, extending the inventions.

Interleaf ranked among the growing throng of companies that were exploiting the power of computers to write, assemble, edit, and print documents. Its engineers had created one of the first commercial "WYSIWYG" user interfaces—a what-you-see-is-what-you-get system, one of the marvels of the time: As you typed, you saw right on your computer screen what the printed page would look like; when you made revisions, they rippled automatically throughout your document.

The company specialized in serving large organizations, selling them the software to create complex, gigantic documents, such as manuals for airplanes. Interleaf had just survived a difficult restructuring of its business. It had about five hundred employees, offices in Europe and Japan, and clients such as Boeing, Caterpillar Tractor, and the U.S. Army.

At one point, a member of the elite team wrote a program to measure the productivity of his colleagues. Paul took on the challenge with relish, and won. He imagined this as friendly competition among peers. But he sometimes uttered angry words about coders he didn't respect. Didn't this person know how to write code? Why didn't Interleaf just eliminate mediocre coders? More than one programmer complained about Paul to Larry Bohn, saying, in effect: "He trashed my code and rewrote it, just to show how good he is." Paul's outbursts didn't seem premeditated to Larry. From time to time, Larry remonstrated with him, and Paul would seem surprised and apologetic. It seemed to Larry that the young man was under the influence of forces he couldn't understand, let alone control.

When Paul arrived, Interleaf was embarking on a large revision of its product. Paul did some of the essential work. He did his coding in a cubicle, sitting for hours and hours in front of a screen, but his mind was a kinetic place, where he was "hauling" code that others had written into his text editor, "grokking it" (scanning and understanding it), and "ripping it apart." Years later, repossessing the young man who did this work, Paul said: "Before I ripped code apart, I first played with it a bit, maybe like some animals play with their prey before eating it."

The existing corpus of Interleaf software consisted of hundreds of thousands of lines of code divided into about two dozen subsystems, such as "pagination" and "tables." Often Paul would make a change in one subsystem and realize he had to make changes in another and then another and another. Sometimes he'd find himself "pushing through" ten subsystems at once, holding the meaning of thousands of lines of code in his mind. It was compelling work. It felt glorious to be at moments the master of a thing so complex. And it was hard to stop. Time went away in stages. "At first, you start to lose track of what time it is. Is it eight P.M. already? You only realize that because you suddenly realize you are incredibly hungry, because you coded right through a mealtime. Then you start losing track of what day of the week it is. In the rare cases where I had to put a date on paper, I sometimes had to think about what month it was. There were many nights when I was coding, so totally enthralled with it that I lost all track of time. I would look at a clock and see four o'clock but have to think for a second as to whether it was 4 P.M. or 4 A.M."

His hundred-hour weeks weren't over when they were over. When he came home to his young wife, it was usually with his thoughts still

framed in the hieroglyphics of the programming languages Lisp and
C, his mind still racing around the Interleaf subsystems. He couldn't
stop talking about his work. He told himself, *I'm just in a prolific
period.* And then there were times when he took a weekend off and
found himself seized with lethargy and unnameable fear, and his
bedroom felt like the nearest thing to a safe place. Once in a while,
he holed up there for an entire day, as he sometimes had in the converted garage on Perham Street. That had probably been a typical
phase of a teenager's life. If so, what was this?

There were days and parts of days when he had to struggle for
civility. This happened most often when he had to go to meetings.
There would be five people in the room and he would try to explain
what he was doing with his code, and no one would understand. He'd
think, *What, are they stupid? How much do I have to spell this out?
They can't go from A to C?* Some of those times he felt as if he were
back in elementary school, teachers asking would he please explain
how he had come up with the answer to a math problem so quickly,
and, feeling both irritated and puzzled, he would reply, "It's obvious." Sometimes in the meeting rooms at Interleaf, it seemed as if
the uncomprehending others were ganging up on him, and what he
felt then was anger. Sometimes he let it show. "Do I have to explain
every fucking step here?"

After about six months of wild coding, Paul forced himself toward
clarity. Something was happening to him that he didn't understand.
It was a weekend. He asked his wife to take him to Newton-Wellesley,
the nearest big hospital. He didn't dare to drive himself.

The neurology resident told Paul that he had bipolar disorder.
Paul didn't want to believe it, but when he returned for a second
opinion, the chief of neurology confirmed the diagnosis and prescribed lithium. The drug left a bad taste in Paul's mouth, as if he'd
been sucking on pennies, and taking the drug meant acknowledging

that he had this thing, this *disorder,* inside him. He told no one at work.

He stayed on lithium for several months, just long enough, almost, to forget how he had felt before. A friend came by his cubicle and asked, "What's wrong with you?"

"Nothing," Paul replied.

"You've lost all your energy," his friend said. "You sure you're not depressed?"

"Actually, I feel pretty flat," said Paul. "Like, I feel safe."

But afterward, he thought, *I don't want to lose my energy.* He could deal with anything but that. He quit lithium at once.

5

INTERLEAF'S OFFICES OCCUPIED FOUR FLOORS, WITH THE EXECU-
tives up top and the programmers at the bottom. You descended
from a land of suits and dresses, potted plants, and sparkling clean
desks, through an intermediate layer of ordinary decor, and finally
arrived at software-engineering world, a crowded warren of cubicles
and offices, with equipment and cardboard boxes scattered here and
there. It was a place where you might pass a dog lying in a doorway,
encounter a young man padding down a hallway in bare feet, spot a
fish tank in a cubicle, startle at the squawk of a parrot from behind
an office door.

Brenda White had started work on an upper floor, in accounts
payable. She was in her twenties, a small, trim woman with warm
brown eyes. She had gone to college at the main UMass campus in
Amherst and had taken some programming courses there. She had
liked them but ended up majoring in economics. She didn't much
care for the subject or her job, but the boss of Interleaf told her that
if she stuck it out in accounting for six months, she could pick her

next assignment. One day in the cafeteria, she overheard a conversation among programmers. They sounded interesting. When her six months were up, she ventured, partly on a hunch, all the way downstairs to engineering.

At first Brenda worked as an assistant to the head of engineering services, a former philosophy major and part-time musician named Joe Mahoney, known informally as the vice president of vocabulary. Under Joe, Brenda began to make a new beginning as a coder. She found a manual for Lisp, and every programmer she asked for help seemed happy to oblige. Soon she was writing small programs in Lisp to automate Joe's email and several of his administrative chores, all to Joe's surprise. Her code was clever, he thought, not the sort of thing you'd expect from someone hired as an entry-level accountant. Why had she written it? "Why wouldn't I?" she replied. "It makes my life easier." Her cheekiness delighted Joe. "Defensive, wiseass wit," he remembered thinking. "She's probably got a one-fifty IQ. She's an autodidact."

Joe had created and was running Interleaf's quality assurance team, a group of engineers who tested the programmers' code. Brenda volunteered to be a QA engineer. She took to the work at once. She felt she had a knack for it. Women had played crucial roles in the creation of the computer age, but by this time there wasn't much in the way of women's equality anywhere in hardware or software companies, or in the classrooms that fed them. On many scores, Interleaf was more progressive than most. But even at Interleaf it was mostly men who wrote code and women who tested it. One executive described quality assurance engineers as "handmaidens."

Brenda would have raised her eyebrows at the notion. She was working among many brilliant programmers, in a role that often made her feel like a student—a student on her way to becoming a connoisseur of code, rating what she read by the relative absence of bugs in a program, the ease with which the code allowed bugs to be fixed, how much space the code took up, how well the parts of a program meshed with each other, how easy the whole thing was to grok. After a while she could study a piece of code and know which of several programmers had written it. Reading a well-wrought subroutine felt at times like going to an art museum. "My body just reacts to it," she'd say. She didn't consider herself an expert judge, but the best coders at Interleaf were heroes to her. Outside of work, Brenda sometimes heard the tribe of software engineers labeled "nerdy," and she would think, *But we're doing such cool things*—things like WYSIWYG interfaces and automatic pagination, which touched and improved the lives of people using their software, and always new things to come.

The programmers struck her as remarkably open and honest: "They just want to solve a problem, and in a clean way. They're creative and sort of innocent." And yet they also seemed very sophisticated.

Her father had died when she was a baby. Her mother had remarried, and Brenda had grown up in an amalgamated family of six kids. They weren't poor, but six children had meant a tight budget, which had meant for instance that she had to go to the state university, where tuition was relatively low. (She remembered her mother telling her, "You can apply to any college you want, but you're going to UMass.")

In Brenda's family, even bagels had been exotic—"Jewish food." Now she was in Cambridge, going out to lunch from time to time with engineers and discovering there was such a thing as Indian cuisine and that she liked it. She had suffered some anxiety as a child and teenager, chiefly the occasional but frightening feeling that she was watching life from a distance, not just other people but herself as well. She felt she couldn't talk about this to her parents or her siblings, and when she tried to tell friends they were simply puzzled, which was worse because it made her feel like an oddity. No one she had known in school or college went to a therapist, not so far as she knew. But here at Interleaf engineering, she often heard colleagues talk openly about their disorders. They'd end conversations saying, "I have therapy. I gotta go," just as if there was nothing to be ashamed of in visiting a therapist. She had never heard people upstairs in sales and marketing talk about therapy. Down here, she even met people who talked openly about being gay.

In Joe Mahoney's regime, most of the anointed coders, the members of the elite team, were assigned their own QA engineer. The best pairings married their professional identities. In a few cases, the relationship turned into an actual marriage. But when the young engineer Paul English arrived and Joe assigned Brenda to work with him, romance was off the table. Paul was happily married and so was Brenda—very happily married to a building contractor, a generous man with legions of friends, whose number soon included Paul. (Paul would say, "He's the guy that if you broke down at three in the morning and you're in Providence and it's January and it's icy rain, you want to have his number in your cellphone.")

Brenda hadn't heard anything about Paul. She knew only that he would be writing a lot of the new Lisp code for the big revision of Interleaf's software, called Active Documents. She looked forward to working more deeply with Lisp and to searching for bugs in the code of another hotshot programmer. This felt in part like a game, a friendly competition—the "scrappy UMass grad," as she thought of herself, finding bugs in the code of guys with "cred," with advanced degrees in programming. It was wonderful, triumphant fun to sit down with a programmer who thought his code was perfect and say to him, "Oh, really? But what about this?"

At first her job was to write bits of code that would test the much more complex code that Paul was writing. She would type up her test code on her computer, send it to Paul, and then join him in his cubicle, three head-high walls enclosing a table. All the engineers named their computers—like pets, Brenda thought. The CTO, Steve Pelletier, named his machine Mulch. She called hers Spanky. And Paul's, as ever, was Speed. He'd bring up both his code and hers and place them side-by-side on Speed's screen. She always enjoyed the times when her test code made his code malfunction, when she could point at the two sets of code on the screen and say, "I found this problem. Why isn't this working?" He always took it well, but in truth this didn't happen often. He wrote very solid code, she thought. Sometimes, she'd deliver the cheery news of a bug and he would peer at the screen and say, "Yes, I accept the fact you found problems with my code, and I'll fix those, but let's look at your code." She didn't feel he was saying, "Your code has problems, too," but rather, "Let me show you something." Invariably, he praised her for her efforts.

As the work progressed, she began to write more substantial programs, to test the concept behind Active Documents. She was the very first person writing in this new system. When she got stuck, she'd go to Paul's cubicle for help. She would explain what she was trying to do. And Paul would stare for a moment at her program on Speed's screen, and then he would put his fingers on his keyboard and something astonishing would happen. The word that came to her mind was "whirlwind."

Like all members of his guild, Paul used "chorded" keyboard commands. To save a document, for instance, you don't bother with a cumbersome mouse. You press a finger down on one of the computer's nonalphanumeric keys, such as Option or Control, and with another finger you hit the S key. Paul had added at least one hundred chorded keyboard commands to his editing program. Partly thanks to them, he typed fast—120 words a minute, by his own calculation. And he wasn't just copying out a term paper. He was inventing complicated software.

Brenda would watch as his fingers flew around the keyboard, her lines of code vanishing from the screen and his new lines appearing. When he finished—rarely more than ten minutes later—she would return to her own desk and study his revision. "Oh, I see why he did that."

Irritability often accompanies hypomania, but Paul almost never felt it when he was "keyboarding up" with someone else, and he never turned it on Brenda. She was an eager and diligent student, she was his partner, and she was very clever. He had long since noticed that she was nice to look at. She didn't wear makeup, at least so far as he could tell. She was pretty, certainly, and to most appearances confident, but he sensed something wounded in her. Maybe the circumstances—their both being newly married—freed him from any feelings of sexual attraction.

One day, he or Brenda—neither could remember which—made a remark about having grown up in a big Catholic family. They compared notes. They started swapping stories. He'd tell a story about one of his brothers, maybe Danny's bottle rocket device. She'd say, "You think that's bad?" and then tell a story of her own. Funny stories soon gave way to sadder ones, and to a sense that they had both been sensitive kids with harried parents, in families too large to serve their particular needs, families in which, as Brenda would say, "It was like, just suck it up, take an aspirin."

This was the beginning of a long conversation. When Brenda brought her code to Paul in his cubicle, they talked about programming mainly. But they went out to lunch about once a week, and then they often shared their stories about anxiety, panic, depression. Paul didn't tell her about his diagnosis, but he described the hopelessness that sometimes settled over him—how on some nights he would sit by a window, looking out for hours, feeling paralyzed, waiting for the sun to free him. Most people she knew kept problems like that secret, usually out of shame, she thought. Here was someone willing to tell her, even sometimes with tears in his eyes, about his pain. It was a gift, and she returned it, telling him about her times of feeling separated from herself and everyone around her. No one had ever understood how much those feelings scared her, but Paul clearly did. He would listen, he was always interested. Brenda thought, "He gets that part of me." Before she'd married her husband, she had found it necessary to ask a girlfriend if he was handsome. Paul probably also fit "in the category of a handsome man," but that didn't matter. "I was so happy in my marriage," she later said. "And it didn't ever even occur to me that, Oh my God, maybe I should be with *this* man. It was more like, I feel so happy to have met somebody who's felt this kind of terror that mental issues can present to you." For his part, Paul thought Brenda was one of the most introspective people he'd ever met, and for that reason "fascinating."

When someone new arrived, Paul, she noticed, often talked as if he'd never met such a splendid person before, and within a week or a month someone else would arrive and fall into what she called Paul's spotlight. She told him he had "a pedestal complex." She wondered if she would fall off. He gave her no reason to think so, but their circumstances began to change. In 1991, about two years after she and Paul started working together, Joe Mahoney and some other executives left the company. In the reorganization, Paul became a manager. Meanwhile, Brenda had her first child. After her leave, she came to the office occasionally, but mostly she worked part-time from home. She and Paul still checked in on each other. He would ask her, "How you doin'?" She knew the question wasn't idle. But she saw him less and less. She didn't regret having children, far from it, but she did look fondly on her first years among programmers and on her sessions with Paul. "I lost my coding buddy," she would say. "It was sad."

6

IN LATER YEARS, PAUL WAS OFTEN ASKED TO TELL HIS SUCCESS story to business students—for instance, at MIT, which had a course in entrepreneurship called "The Founder's Journey." Paul's journey upward began at Interleaf, where the CTO, Steve Pelletier, recognized a quality that removed Paul from the ranks of most programmers. The best of them, Pelletier had found, could keep entire complex schemes in mind. But only a few could look beyond the code itself and see its "meta content," its place in a company's strategy, its likely effects on customers and sales. Early on, Pelletier thought he spotted that rare ability, "a superb meta sense," in Paul. Other executives agreed. Paul had "management potential."

Does programming attract strange people, or does it make them strange? Either way, a coder moving into management is apt to find the transition hard. A friend of Paul's put the matter this way: "Eventually, if programmers are successful, they rise and have to deal with people." Paul was first made a product leader, not managing people exactly, but coordinating the work of five other programmers. Soon he took a scunner to one of the team and complained to Larry Bohn, who told him: "Paul, you need her. Someone has to do the work you don't want to do."

Bouts of hypomania didn't help. On a day after Paul had been promoted, one of the elite programmers approached Joe Mahoney and said of Paul, "I half expect to see him come out of the bathroom with green lithium powder around his lips."

Mahoney was puzzled. He didn't even know what lithium was. "What are you talking about?" he said.

"When he's in a really good mood and he's around a bunch of people and he's doing a bunch of really positive stuff, you just watch him. A week later he's gonna whack someone."

Mahoney replied, "You're full of shit. What is this? Your fucking armchair psychological shit?" And afterward, of course, Mahoney couldn't help but start to watch his young friend. Soon enough he saw the pattern for himself—cheerful, enthusiastic Paul in a sudden fury, dressing down one of his team. "Don't you know how to write code? This stuff is crap!"

Nonetheless, Paul's bosses kept offering him promotions. He resisted. He didn't want to run meetings or deal with other coders' problems. He wanted to go on writing code. But then his wrists began to ache. He began to imagine they were bleeding within. He visited a doctor, who diagnosed carpal tunnel syndrome and suggested surgery. Real management seemed like the only alternative.

His idea of managing at that point required that he write some code, but only in bursts, short enough to be endurable and necessary, for the simple reason that he didn't know another way to do the job. When he disagreed with others on his little team, he would begin by drawing diagrams on a whiteboard and criticizing their approaches. He thought of this as "beating up their code." And when they ganged up on him, insisting that his solution would take three weeks to execute, he would stride back to Speed and spend about an hour writing some of the code in question. He called this "coding the proof into existence." He thought of management as "battle." He was bound to win when the odds were only one to five. He could handle ten, though it was hard, especially with aching wrists. But when he was made responsible for fifty, he realized that he had to find new ways of contending.

Can people reinvent themselves? Many must believe they can. Otherwise, the great self-improvement library of America wouldn't keep on growing. Paul had never felt a need for self-help books, but he had a quality of mind that was open to their sort of promise, a quality more generative than reflective, a childlike innocence about impossibility, or at least, as his old friend Karl had noticed, a straight-forward way of facing difficulties: "You see the problem, you solve the problem."

How to manage people when outcoding them no longer sufficed? For the first and only time in his life, Paul turned to books of business advice. One was called *Executive Leadership: A Practical Guide to Managing Complexity*. Another was *SPIN Selling*. The acronym stood for Situation, Problem, Identification, Need. The book was full of advice on ways of promoting one's ideas inside an organization. He went at those and other self-help guides with much the same intensity that he had brought to programming.

Several trained philosophers joined Interleaf in its early years. One was a marketing executive named David Weinberger. He remembered the figure Paul had cut on arrival, a young hotshot developer fairly typical of the breed: "brash, self-confident, ruffling feathers, professionally arrogant." How many years had it been since then? No more than three or four, and Paul was hardly recognizable. He still wore jeans, and he was still extremely energetic. But now, in his elevated role as a manager of managers, Paul seemed judicious, considerate, and even, when necessary, patient. Evidently, others liked to work for him. What had happened? Weinberger felt he had to ask. Paul had become a really talented manager, Weinberger said. How had he done it?

"The brash young developer wasn't working for me anymore," Paul replied. "So I read books and tried to change."

An extraordinary statement, the kind one remembers. "How unusual that is," Weinberger said years later. "To realize that you don't just need to change techniques, but also personality."

Paul wasn't transformed, of course, just modified. He went back on lithium now and then, but he found it easy to quit the drug, and he avoided it most of the time. He still spent some nights awake staring out the bedroom window, and there were still moments when everyone around him seemed too slow to understand him, moments that he spent writhing with impatience. The difference was that he usually managed to hide his anger and to make his points laboriously, going from A to B to C even when the way to C seemed obvious.

As all help-in-business books have promised since Benjamin Franklin, self-improvement paid. Paul became vice president of engineering. In the fourth quarter of 1994, after Interleaf reported a loss of $20 million, the board fired the CEO and made Paul one of a triumvirate temporarily in charge of the entire company. His rise in the hierarchy brought the first international travel of his life—a trip to Germany to make a pitch to Siemens, and two others, even headier, to visit customers in Japan—and it also offered him the chance to negotiate his first taste of wealth. The board wanted the triumvirate to find a new CEO, and they also asked Paul to fix the problems with the product line. But the board had fired the CEO and made these requests before determining Paul's pay, and he took full advantage.

They'd have to give him a salary of $175,000 a year and $2 million in stock options, he said. Otherwise he would quit. In fairly short order, Paul and the two other triumvirs cut the number of vice presidents by half and found a new CEO, who gave Paul a choice of jobs. He could run engineering and all the business units, or, if he liked, he could run marketing. Paul said he didn't know anything about marketing, and the new boss said, "Great. Run marketing." *Why not?* Paul thought. *I'm way over my head already.*

On the face of it, he had become a different creature from the people writing code on the bottom floor. He had become a suit. But the transition was far from complete. From the time when Paul had first joined their ranks, as vice president of engineering, business executives had seemed like an odd bunch to him. *What do these guys do?* he had wondered. They seemed to spend a lot of their time creating jobs for themselves, managers creating a need for management. He would look at the man who was the CEO at the time and tell himself, *Okay, he's a suit. He probably plays a good golf game, probably has a fancy house. Okay, he's different. That doesn't mean he's bad.* Paul would tell himself that programmers and suits were too dismissive of each other, but then he'd go to a meeting in the CEO's conference room and give a presentation about a revision of the Interleaf software and everyone in the room would look puzzled or start glancing out the windows. And then another executive would get up and give what seemed to Paul like an endless, mind-numbing PowerPoint presentation about the company's financials, and all the executives would be nodding at each other and shaking their heads and pursing their lips as if to say, "Good point."

He was a suit who rarely wore a suit, and who thought of himself as a programmer at heart. He tried to keep track of his former compatriots by reading their "release mail," all the notes the programmers wrote when they added code to the system. In this way, he met the young Bill O'Donnell, and was moved as a craftsman might be moved by the work of a newfound peer. The kid, Billo, was a monster coder, a "10X coder," able to do the work of ten, one of the best in the company, Paul thought.

Having ascended to management, Paul wasn't supposed to code anymore, but for a long time he had kept his hand in surreptitiously, working with various programmers. One of them was Schwenk, a youngster then. During their first time of working together, Schwenk really feared the experience would give him an ulcer—emails from Paul coming at all hours, Schwenk misunderstanding many of them, Paul misunderstanding Schwenk's replies, until finally Schwenk worked up his courage and told Paul, "I'm not going to answer emails in the middle of the night anymore."

Paul had also kept in touch with his old classmate Karl Berry, and when the Free Software Foundation had run out of money to pay Karl's salary, Paul had hired him at Interleaf. Among other, more important roles, Karl acted as Paul's personal coder, automating many of Paul's administrative tasks.

Karl did his programming mainly at home. He didn't like meetings. He once said, "I don't want to talk to people. I want to email with them." The arrangement suited Paul. His duties at Interleaf kept him very busy. Email was an efficient and relatively safe means for managing a relationship that mixed business and friendship. Their exchanges were often framed like conversations, between "pme" and "karl," and came with graphic frowns and smiles:

:-(:-)

One day, in an email praising Karl—he was someone who "blind-sides us with awesome/quick solutions" and who "also sends out sharp criticisms/suggestions"—Paul let something slip: "As long as I work here and that will still be a while more, I'll make sure to remove any/all admin/politics from you and to keep your work environment as pleasant as possible." This exchange ensued:

> karl: Uh oh. I know this was supposed to be reassuring, but it has the opposite effect on me! Does this mean the end is in sight?
> pme: No, not in sight.
> karl: I hope you'll take me with you, if possible. :-)
> pme: I certainly will, whenever that is . . .

Whenever came two months later.

> pme: Call me at work today or at home tonight. I need to speak with you.

7

AROUND 1994, PAUL AND BILL O'DONNELL CAME UP WITH AN IDEA
for a utility that would let Interleaf customers create their own webpages. Billo designed and wrote the software. It won a prize, but
when he and Paul presented it to Interleaf's sales force, they were all
but laughed out of the room. One of the salesmen said, "Boeing's not
going to use the *Web*. People have pictures of their cats on the Web."

The sales force wasn't wrong. Only eight million Americans were
connected to the Internet at the time, and most of them used it just
for email. And the Web was all but brand-new, its content very thin.
But the technology represented a vast improvement in the distribu-
tion of electronic documents and thus, potentially, a great enhance-
ment of the Internet. Paul saw unbounded promise in it and in the
growing host of new online technologies. So he was disposed to listen
when, in 1995, the founder of a local Internet-related start-up began
recruiting him.

This was the fledgling company NetCentric. The founder pitched it as a twenty-first-century phone company, its first product facilities for faxing over the Internet. Businesses and law firms all relied on faxing for the rapid exchange of documents, but they were obliged to use telephone lines, and the rates, especially for long-distance transmission, were still high. In principle, NetCentric could offer them a much better deal, because faxes could travel over the Internet for free. Two reputable venture capital firms in Boston had already bet five million on the new company. Paul was offered the job of running engineering, in return for a substantial share of the company's stock.

Only half of his Interleaf stock options had vested. Quitting Interleaf now meant leaving a million dollars behind. He didn't care. The move looked like a sensible step into the future. Once he had made it, it seemed only obvious to ask Billo and Schwenk and a few others to follow him. He soon went to work on Karl as well.

Paul felt strongly about Karl, not just as a friend but as a skilled and trustworthy coder. "Some programmers, if you put them in a room and say, 'Take things coming in the left window and have them go out the right window,' they'll say, 'Sure. But what if I add more windows?' or 'What if there's a dragon that melts the windows?' Karl, if you ask him to do something, he does it."

> pme: Any way we could get you to do a 1-2 (or 3?) week fulltime contract for us?
> karl: I would commit suicide if I tried to do this. Sorry.
> pme: Well, that would certainly defeat the purpose. :-)

Karl did agree to work part-time for Paul, and from home. Paul offered to get him a NetCentric business card.

> karl: I don't want a business card :-).
> pme: So like, do you have a home page yet? You should.

karl: No. I hate the idea. HTML is too limiting; everybody's home
page looks like everyone else's, and I refuse to cooperate :-).
pme: You don't have to cooperate—plenty of room for creativity . . .
I think you should at least create an anti-karl home page, one
depicting the not-you, e.g., "I love driving my BMW through city
traffic . . ." :-)

Paul thought NetCentric was bound to make a fortune, and he
wanted Karl to get a share. Did Karl want to buy some of the stock
that Paul owned? Karl replied, "Yes, I guess so. Although I've never
ventured into such things before."

Other emails on this subject followed:

karl: I'm thinking $10K (remember, I'm poor :-).
pme: How about $5K for now, possibly more later? I think you'll get
an unbelievable return on investment, but there is of course the
chance that we could fall on our faces and you'd lose all of your
money (and me tons more due to huge investments I've made :-).
karl: So this is like gambling. :-)

Karl bought $5,000 worth of Paul's stock, and Paul kept coaxing
him to work full-time at NetCentric.

pme: You'd fit fine. People love you here . . .
karl: They do? It never seems like it.
pme: They do. Really.
karl: I suppose I should at least pretend to care about money :-) . . .
pme: Don't do it for money. Money is a yucky reason to switch
jobs. Decide what is best for your lifestyle and goals right now. I
think we'd probably offer a more stimulating environment, brighter/
passionate people, also more upbeat. Also (if you care), you could

have a chance to work on leading edge technology that *will* have a big impact on millions of people and the net.

About two months later Paul was out of a job.

He got in a fight with NetCentric's boss—over pay for engineers. The boss later insisted that Paul had quit. But Paul felt he had been fired, and he took it very hard.

He emailed Karl the news but none of the details. In all innocence, Karl wrote:

> karl: BTW, not that I'm in any rush about it, but I presume the $5K you let me buy of your stock will be coming back to me now with some minimal interest . . .
>
> pme: I thought about that last night. I feel awkward and am not sure what's the best thing to do . . . I'd *certainly* be happy to do as you suggest, say, send you $6K instead of the $5K you invested. Would that be ok with you? Do you think I'd be being fair? I want to do whatever is the right thing . . . No matter how we decide to resolve this one, I desperately want to work with you again.

The stock Paul owned in NetCentric had no present cash value—and would have no value at all within a few years, when NetCentric went out of business. He had made a lot of money at Interleaf, though, and had saved enough to live on for a year or two at least. What he lacked was a purpose. By now he had traded in his first house in Arlington for a much larger one. He had made an office in a corner of its attic, stuffy with the scent of old unpainted wood. The only natural light came from a pair of small windows under the eaves. He had a chair, a couple of tables, computing equipment. He spent a lot of time up there in the days after he left NetCentric, voyaging out into the land of the Internet while seated under the rafters, and writing cheerful-seeming emails to Karl about possible new enterprises.

It wasn't hard to put on a brave face for Karl. They met almost exclusively by computer, after all. In fact, Paul was in a bad way. He had talked Billo and Schwenk and Karl and others into following him to NetCentric, and he had let them down. He had reason to feel depressed, in the ordinary sense of the word. But this was something different. This was the other side of mania, despair out of all proportion to whatever brought it on, to any apparent cause. It didn't allow him to feel that he'd simply had a setback. It insisted on his worst fears. *Maybe I'm not supposed to be a VP of engineering. Maybe I'm just incompetent.*

The undercurrent of such thoughts was composed of gloom and lassitude and fearfulness, at times panic, and it felt like something deep and wide moving inside him, like a chemical flood. He tried to hide his distress from his family, but of course there was no hiding it from his wife. She did all she could to help him. She was always sympathetic, struggling to comfort him. But he felt sick beyond all help, a state of mind that all but guaranteed the fact.

He wasn't taking lithium, nor did he go back on it again. Many nights he couldn't sleep for more than a few hours. During some he couldn't lie in bed. A bed seemed too insubstantial. While his family slept, he would climb out and crawl across the floor toward a window, crawling because he felt the need for something solid under him. He'd lie there for hours, watching for the sun to appear above the sill. Afterward, he would remember telling himself, *This cloud's going to lift sooner or later. It may take a year, but it will lift.* The sun was the evidence he counted on. Even though on some nights the wait seemed perpetual, one knew after all that the sun would rise and then there would be forward movement in the world, promising relief.

Paul had long practiced his own form of adult education, partly trying to make up for his truancy at Boston Latin but mostly out of a curiosity that ranged from rap music to international medicine to fine arts. He had read about bipolar disorder ever since receiving his diagnosis, and he had determined that he wasn't one of those especially prone to suicide. He knew he'd never kill himself. In the past when he had lain awake like this, staring out windows, he had sometimes summoned up an image drawn from high school English class. He was Gulliver imprisoned by the tiny Lilliputians, laid out on his back, tied to the ground with a web of tiny ropes. In his mind, he would roll his shoulders from side to side, and eventually, after long exertions, one of the ropes would snap, then another and another.

———————

One day up in the attic, memories of playing xiangqi, Chinese chess, floated into Paul's mind. The World Wide Web hadn't existed when he had first discovered the game at UMass. He looked to see if you could now play online and he found a xiangqi club, not a website, just a link to a program that would let two people play each other. It had been created by a couple of Chinese graduate students at Boston University.

He wrote to Karl, asking for help in setting up something much better. His emails were buoyant. "Xiang Qi (chinese chess) is the most popular game in the world, with an estimated 500,000,000 people who know how to play it," he wrote. "I think there's a very good chance that with little work, we could setup the #1 web service for the #1 game in the world." It would also provide a public service: "I'm eager to have westerners learn about this game—anything that can increase cultural exchange is a good thing."

Karl's reply was guarded. What had happened to Paul's other ideas?

Paul replied, "I decided that I work too hard in general, and deserve a sabbatical before launching into something full force." Setting up xiangqi for the Web would be "a lower impact effort," and almost certainly turn out to be "a neat little profitable venture."

All this sounded like the optimistic Paul, the only Paul Karl knew. While writing this way, Paul could believe he was on the verge of getting back in the game of software commerce. But inevitably such a cheery thought summoned up its opposite, and he would think of how far he had fallen—from executive suites and million-dollar stock options and hundreds of people reporting to him, to a lonely seat in an attic, chasing fantasies.

And yet this new adventure had intrinsic appeal. The xiangqi board and pieces had been for Paul an introduction to an ancient and artistic culture, and they still seemed wonderfully fanciful.

A river divides the two halves of the xiangqi board; crossing it, pawns acquire added powers. There are two kings, but the rules confine them and their counselors to their respective palaces, a section of squares marked off on opposite sides of the board. The horse, roughly equivalent to a knight, is said to be "hobbled" when certain configurations of adjacent pieces prevent it from moving. There are chariots and cannons—the Chinese name for the cannon sounds like "Pow," which delighted Paul.

Xiangqi was like a magic carpet. While he rode it, the dreary attic disappeared. Long days and nights were shortened. Over the next two months, as New England's springtime arrived—invisible through the slits of windows under the eaves—details of the website assembled in his mind. It was like a place in a dream, like a vision he received, a little pleasure dome for modern lovers of xiangqi. In this vision, members of a Worldwide Xiangqi League would come from near and far to gather at Club Xiangqi. They would sign up, gratis, and choose their playing names, and then each would receive a password and a special league email address for staying in touch with members and administrators. Each would also get a special webpage. You could open yours and look at the list of all your past games and order up replays. Looking for a game? You'd enter the lobby and take a look at the names and ratings—from novice to expert—of other unpaired players, including "robots," xiangqi-playing programs. When you found an opponent, you would order a game room, each equipped with the finest of boards, colorfully painted. On the screen, the pieces, disks three-dimensionally rendered with their Chinese characters painted in red, were going to be imbued with the vigor that players like his Vietnamese friends at UMass had given them. When you moved a piece, it would bounce to its new place, emitting the champagne-cork pop. When you took one of your opponent's pieces and removed it from the board, that slap-slap of wood on wood would resound as if to say, "Take that!" You could play unrecorded practice rounds, or, if you only wanted to watch, you could go into the lobby, consult the list of games in progress, then enter your chosen room. Trusted players, "coaches," would have commands at their disposal for curbing bad behavior. A "Ban" command would allow them to expunge the chronically, egregiously obnoxious.

When Paul left the xiangqi palace and looked around his attic, he would be reminded once again that only a month ago he'd been the VP of a hot new tech start-up. But at times up there under the rafters, transported into the realm of xiangqi, he became a leader with an idea for an enterprise and a little team to enact it. At first this team included the Boston University grad students, but eventually they had to leave for paying jobs, and then the team was only he and Karl. Periodically, Paul would write to Karl that he was courting financiers, assuring Karl that someday they'd get paid for creating this site. One time, Paul offered Karl a token payment of a thousand dollars, Karl wrote that it wasn't necessary, Paul sent the check anyway, and Karl wrote, "Gee, thanks."

Karl had left Interleaf and had another paying job. He had some time to spare, and he'd always liked to work with Paul. Paul was so energetic and generous, his management style so different from the bureaucratic, rule-bound norm. By summer he and Paul had put together a functioning, though rudimentary, website. Karl wrote the administrative programs. Paul, meanwhile, was planning to write new foundations for their site—a big coding job.

In better days, Paul had bought a summer house in Hull, larger than his parents' cottage and situated on the shore of Massachusetts Bay. In mid-June he and his wife and two small children moved there for the summer. For Paul and indeed all the English family, Hull had always felt more like home than Perham Street. Hull was the place where he and Danny had done their most inventive mischief, the place where he had felt a part of a truly happy family. He knew the history of the town and of the harbor islands in its panorama. Every upstairs room of the house commanded lovely views, boats on blue waters, the grand old Boston Light, and in the distance to the west across Boston Harbor, the towers of the financial district. There were times of relief this summer, when for instance he took the ferry to Boston and returned to find his infant son and daughter and wife waiting for him at the terminal in Hull, and his heart lifted. Or the times when he made chocolate cake, his daughter standing on the counter covered in flour. But the main escape from the gloom that lingered in Paul's mind lay on his computer screen.

In moving to Hull, Paul had traded his attic office for a basement room. It was barely large enough for a desk and a couple of tables to hold computing gear. Down there, all that Paul could sense of the oceanfront world came through a small window near the top of one wall, high above eye level, which he had installed to replace an even smaller window with a rotten frame. The room had a concrete floor, usually damp, and the place smelled musty, like the converted garage on Perham Street. There at his desk in the basement, with just a patch of sunlight or moonlight in the window above his head, the dank little room seemed to him like a fair representation of the feelings that kept returning, his interior darkness made tangible.

Emails to Karl still read like descriptions of how Paul wished he felt. He and Karl were going to learn everything "soup to nuts" about what it took to make a good website. Theirs was sure to be a hit.

The sound in Paul's mind was much more tentative. The challenge he had set himself, and had postponed for some months, was to rewrite from scratch two large programs, the new foundation of code for the xiangqi gaming palace. It had been a long time since he'd done a coding job this large and complicated. Could he do it? *Can I create again? I'm not sure I can create again.* But when he sat down at his computer in his basement office, on a day in July, he knew—it was reflexive—just how and where to start.

Some coders draw diagrams of their programs before they begin to write them. Paul had never felt the need. He'd always been able to hold a large, complex construction in his mind. His picture of the two programs was like a map of all their parts and the connections among them. A kinetic map. He loved populous Manhattan avenues. Imagined from above, they were like an efficient program, he thought, the crowds moving in opposing currents and crosscurrents that never quite touched, that seldom interfered with each other.

Donald Knuth once said, "Computer scientists seem to have an uncanny ability to jump between levels of abstraction—to see things 'in the small' while at the same time seeing them 'in the large.'" Paul could still do this. He could still write something like a cascade of coded routines, each hanging from the one above, like a Calder mobile.

As the programs took shape on his screen, he felt more and more nearly obsessed with this odd adventure at every level of abstraction, as in the old days at Interleaf and before Interleaf. He still lay awake in the middle of many nights, but he wasn't huddled on the floor waiting for the sun. He was lying in bed thinking about the code he had written and the code still to write, or he was down in the basement with the lights on, writing it. This wouldn't be the road to mental health for most people, but for him it felt more and more like a way back, a new beginning.

By September, when he and his family returned to Arlington, the bulk of the two programs was written: about 10,000 lines of code, which, if printed out, would fill about 170 dense and very neat-looking pages. There had been much more prodigious feats of programming, but this was a large job for one person to have accomplished in about two and a half months.

I still have it, he told himself. *I still have my chops.*

———

The Club Xiangqi caught the attention of a few companies, including Yahoo. One of its founders came to Boston and talked about buying both the site and Paul. Yahoo made him a handsome offer, and Paul wanted to accept it, but the company was situated in California, and he couldn't move there and leave most of his extended family. For a time he thought he was slipping back toward despair. The world was going mad for people who knew how to create things for the Internet, and for a while he felt stuck outside looking in. He still had money in the bank, but it was ebbing. He worked briefly as a part-time programmer for a small company, earning $80 an hour, thinking again of how far he had fallen, thinking, as he sat in a cubicle making boring repairs to badly written code, *My normal self would rewrite all of this.*

But his gloom didn't last long this time. Soon after he turned down Yahoo, he had a chance encounter, on a Massachusetts golf course, of all places—he could scarcely play the game—where he met a man who was working for *The Boston Globe*, managing the paper's online store. Soon afterward Paul had a deal to improve the *Globe*'s website, to make it a place where visitors could easily buy all sorts of Boston-related stuff, such as T-shirts and snow globes and sports team paraphernalia. The contract was for $50,000, a contract for a product before Paul had a company to build it. He had a name, though—Boston Light Software.

If all went well, he'd assemble a great team and they'd build Boston Light into a website creator that would serve all sorts of giant corporations, once they'd done their first job for the *Globe*. He imagined that he and Karl would make good use of their Xiangqi experience, not the actual code they'd written but what they had learned about creating a complicated site on the Web.

He felt proud of what he and Karl had done, constructing out of the ephemeral stuff of code what seemed like a real community, indeed a real place where tens of thousands of people all over the world were hanging out electronically and competing and learning the game of xiangqi. He liked to go to the club himself and enter a room to watch a game, and if a player in Malaysia made a bad move, it was as if Paul could hear his fellow spectators—one might be in Japan, another in China—murmuring: "Can you believe he did that?"

Paul felt that Xiangqi had saved him from despair. But he had been spending fifty to sixty hours a week on the Xiangqi League, and none of his dreams of making money from it had materialized. He had two houses and a wife and young children. He had taken a step back to a former self. He had programmed his way out of depression. Now it was time to go back to work.

8

WHEN PAUL FOUNDED BOSTON LIGHT—IN 1998, THREE YEARS
after he quit Interleaf—impermanence had become the norm, new
inventions displacing ones that only yesterday seemed new, computer-
related businesses forming and dying, flourishing and dissolving and
being bought for their patents, or disappearing, as Interleaf was soon
to do, into other companies. The latest craze now was business on the
Internet. Part of the promise lay in the old idea of making money
through advertising. The medium was new, though, and so were the
terms for it: e-commerce, information technology, the tailored Web
experience, dot-coms, all amounting to nothing less than a New Economy.

Virtually all the dot-coms listed their shares on the NASDAQ
exchange. That index doubled between 1999 and March 2000. One
estimate has it that in the midst of the boom the value of the 371
publicly traded Internet companies amounted to $1.3 *trillion*, about
8 percent of the value of all the stock traded in the United States.

To take another measure of the era, the number of venture capital firms—many "VCs" specialized in financing new dot-coms—also nearly doubled between 1996 and 1999, and the capital they had to spend grew threefold, from about $50 billion to more than $160 billion. In retrospect, these amounted to clear symptoms of a bubble. Some people involved in the financial markets saw trouble coming, but in finance as in technology, being right too soon is as punishing as being right too late. Even some wary investors felt they had to follow the herd or risk a fatal loss of reputation, or at least of opportunity.

In the context of that period's economy—manic, not just hypomanic—Paul's Boston Light was a model of sanity. He had a paying customer and something like a business plan—to make handsome and reliable websites for all sorts of companies. He didn't even try to raise money from outside investors. Making software didn't require anything like the capital involved in manufacturing. He figured he had enough to open the doors of Boston Light with the $50,000 from the *Globe* and what remained of his savings.

He rented an office in Arlington, the cheapest space he could find. It had no cleaning service and the heat was unreliable, but it cost only $8 a square foot. He fitted it out with used furniture and bought some new server computers. He recruited a team of fifteen, a couple of smart young businesspeople, support staff, and programmers. Most of these were old colleagues—such as the versatile programmer and manager Jim Giza, and also Karl, who would take care of the smooth operation of the company's systems. It was a big moment for Paul when Billo agreed to abandon his little start-up. When Schwenk and Rago followed, Paul felt he had the team he needed. He couldn't afford to pay them much, but for Billo and others there was the promise of adventure and money to come.

When Paul called asking Brenda to join Boston Light, she told him, "Yes. If I can work part-time." Paul said she could, then put her in charge of creating the UI for the *Globe*'s website, a more than full-time job. But to be working long hours among old friends, at communal tables in one big open room, felt like a return to what she thought of as her "glory days." Karl was one of those old friends. She remembered asking back in Interleaf days why he kept wearing the same old wool sweater with holes in its sleeves, and Karl had told her his mother had given it to him and he was damned if he was going to replace it. It made her happy to see that he was still wearing it when she saw him again, for the first time in years, at Boston Light.

Paul made Karl a co-founder of the new company and endowed him with about a quarter of the stock, about half as much as Paul took for himself.

> karl: It seems bizarre that I have so much. I could conceivably give some up if it seems appropriate.
> pme: Please don't ever suggest that; you are *well* worth all the stock you have. It is very important to me personally (and the company) for you to be positive, and to feel good about your value here. I think if you felt >=50% as good about your value here as I felt about your value here, you'd be in good shape. :-)

It wasn't a calculated feeling, but clearly Paul wanted Karl around for something in addition to his expertise and trustworthiness, something more intangible. Karl hewed to his countercultural ideals— his scorn for the restrictions on freedom that the capitalist system wanted to place on programmers in the form of patents and other legal devices. This made him vulnerable in a world that cared for little more than money. He was someone Paul felt he could protect, someone on whose behalf Paul could practice his own idealism.

At one point, Paul asked Karl to sign a standard employment agreement. But Karl objected to a section of the document that would prevent him from working on the same kinds of projects as those at Boston Light for a year, if he should leave the company.

> pme: . . . It is too late for us to make changes, we really do need you to sign it. Please take a leap of faith for me and just sign it as is, ok?

The exchange continued:

> pme: . . . You have to sign it.
> karl: No, I do not have to sign it. I will quit before I sign it as it stands. I will give you all the stock back.
> pme: There is no need to escalate like this; threats are not nice, they don't show trust and beg for further escalation.
> karl: It is not a threat and it has nothing to do with trust.
> pme: It was a pretty powerful suggestion. :-)
> karl: I trust you absolutely.
> pme: Thank you; it makes me feel 1000% better. Trust is everything to me. :-) There must be a way we can do this . . .

And of course there was a way, essentially a promise from Paul that he would never enforce the clause. Karl approved of the compromise. He would not feel his principles had been violated. He added:

> (This is of course completely an ethical/philosophical question on my part, not "practical." I can't imagine having the slightest interest or capability of starting or joining an ecommerce company after boston light.)

Karl liked working with Paul as much as ever. For one thing, Paul would let him work remotely. "I think you overestimate the power of talking face-to-face," Karl wrote him on one occasion, adding, "(And I know you think I underestimate it.)" Early on Paul did ask Karl to come in and look at the office. "Okay. Whatever," Karl said. He had to set up the server computers from scratch. He didn't care what the office looked like, only that the machine room, his province, be suitable. He looked at it. It was large enough to work in comfortably. "Okay, I'm happy." Once he had the machines set up, Karl resumed working mostly at home, visiting the office only now and then, talking mainly with Paul by email.

> pme: I would really like to get cards for you, for when/if we are in meetings, and so your not getting cards is not seen as not being supportive of the team or something.
> karl: If you insist, but I'll never use them.
> pme: You can make up card games with them. What title do you want?
> karl: "Programmer." If you veto that, Co-founder.
> pme: Ok.

In a fairly typical early email to his managers, Paul announced exciting dot-com news, followed by an exhortation:

> AOL market cap doubled this week to $62B . . .
> This is fucking unreal.
> Their valuation is based on the number of consumers they have.
> If there's anything for us to learn from this, it is that everything we do should be focused on only one goal—
> MAXIMIZE THE NUMBER OF SHOPPERS (and merchants) in 1999
> THAT WILL USE BLS SOFTWARE . . .

The zeitgeist was with him. Software entrepreneurs, he wrote, were standing "in the middle of a hurricane."

If you were a corporate manager at this time, you had to get a website built for your company. If you didn't, your business might not suffer right away, but your company's stock price certainly would. Paul figured he could talk a lot of companies, large and small, into hiring his team to create their sites. He had several friendly conversations, with a couple of hot young Internet companies, with Amazon, and with Intuit, a large and growing software company that provided tools for small businesses and accountants. None of those companies, Paul began to realize, wanted to buy Boston Light's services, but all, to one degree or another, expressed some interest in buying him and his team. He preferred Intuit because it was the only one of the suitors that was actually making money—$800 million in revenue and $386 million in profit in 1999.

Paul wasn't opposed to selling. He had stretched himself financially, a little with the Xiangqi adventure and a lot with Boston Light. Paying more than a dozen salaries had consumed his Interleaf money. He had sold all the investments in his pension plan. He was nearly broke, nearly "out of liquids," and on the verge of turning to credit-card financing. He didn't feel desperate, but that didn't mean the situation wasn't desperate. When he felt the fire, being in a jam brought a kind of happiness. It eliminated distractions. It settled him. Whatever the jam, he felt sure he'd find a way out. This time he had help, in the person of his old friend Joe Mahoney, "the vice president of vocabulary," from Interleaf days.

Joe was working in Massachusetts as an adviser to Intuit. At Joe's suggestion, the company dispatched a small team to visit Boston Light. They weren't ready to buy. They told Joe Mahoney that they liked Paul and his team but not the software they were building. Mahoney told them to forget the software, the prize was Paul. "This is a sui generis individual," Joe remembered saying. "He is a completely unique guy. He can think decisively, omnivorously, in ways that you guys haven't seen before. And here's a chance to get *him* on our team, not just his technology."

Mahoney arranged to have Paul join a phone conference about a start-up company that Intuit was thinking of buying. That start-up's young founder gave his pitch by phone to a scattered panel of judges: the Intuit executives in Mountain View, California, and Mahoney in his office in his house in Brookline, outside Boston, and Paul, who was sitting downstairs on an extension phone in Mahoney's kitchen.

When the young founder finished his pitch and hung up, the others all stayed on the line, offering their opinions. And then it was Paul's turn, his audition. He didn't talk long. ("The succession of it was almost miraculous," Mahoney remembered.) Paul told them what he thought was right and wrong about the company in question. He raised issues that no one else on the call had considered. He didn't tell the Intuit people what to do but left them feeling that the decision was clear (they shouldn't buy).

The Intuit team was suitably impressed, enough that Intuit invested about two million in Boston Light and soon afterward decided to buy it. But what was the market value of a company only a little more than six months old, with fifteen employees and an unfinished first product? Paul heard that another old colleague from Interleaf had just negotiated the sale of a small new company. Paul called him for advice. The old friend asked him how much he planned to ask. Paul said he wasn't sure. Maybe twenty million? Ask for forty, his friend said. *Forty?* Paul said. Boston Light didn't have any revenue, said Paul, except for fifty grand from *The Boston Globe*. His friend said to ask for forty million anyway. You could argue that this was a modest price, in the context of the moment. In 1999, a year of many buyouts, Yahoo agreed to pay $3.6 billion of its own overvalued stock for GeoCities, a very popular online "community," and $6.1 billion for Broadcast.com, an Internet radio company that owned no content and produced audio and video of poor quality. Neither of those companies had ever made any money or even come very close to breaking even, and the same was true of most of the dozens of smaller dot-coms that were getting bought or going public.

The Intuit negotiator was a woman. Paul liked her. He considered her a formidable adversary. He thought of her as "cigar-smoking, whiskey-drinking, tough." As Paul remembered, she said, "Are you fucking *kidding* me? Forty million for that piece of shit?" She hung up on him.

Paul called her back.

"Forty, that's crazy," she said.

He said, "I agree. I'm probably worth a hundred thousand, but the market thinks I'm worth more, and I'm negotiating right now with four other companies."

Karl was working at home when he received not an email but an actual phone call from Paul. This meant something important was up, or anyway something Paul thought was important. "You ought to come in to work today," Paul said.

"Why?" asked Karl.

"Just come," Paul said, and when Karl arrived, Paul told him, "We're going for a drive." A drive to nowhere, so Paul could talk out of earshot of the other employees. "Intuit's agreed to acquire us for thirty-three and a half million dollars," said Paul.

"Well," said Karl. "What does this mean? What happens next?"

Paul said they'd have a company meeting and announce the sale, but right now he and Karl had to figure out who should get bonuses. In the car, Paul started naming the employees, beginning with Billo, whose share of the stock was tiny compared to Paul's, compared to Karl's. Paul said it wasn't enough. Karl agreed emphatically. They went through the list. "This is weird," Karl said. "Why don't we give everybody a bonus?"

"Great idea. Let's do it!" said Paul.

They decided to cut their own shares in half—Paul's $16 million reduced to $8 million, Karl's $8 million to $4 million—and spread that money around among the others. When they announced this at the office, one of the beneficiaries asked, "And you're doing this why? Because you're communists or something?"

"Right," said Paul, and Karl felt like applauding.

Paul's next stop was Hull. His family had moved down there for the summer, and so had his parents, with their toaster. They were visiting at Paul's house when Paul arrived. It was evening, and his father was sitting on the porch, taking in the sea air, facing out across the water toward Boston. He was an old man now, white-haired and, quite unlike his once forceful self, a bit fearful of the world. Paul had always felt wary of seeming boastful around him, but he simply had to tell him what he'd done. "I sold my company, Dad."

His father smiled. But when Paul told him the price—"Thirty-three and a half million, Dad"—the old man's smile vanished. He glanced quickly from side to side. This was the man who once prided himself on never seeming fazed. *It's like he thinks the FBI is going to show up any minute,* Paul thought.

"Who negotiated for you?" his father asked.

"I did," said Paul.

"You didn't have a lawyer do it?"

"No."

"How do *you* know about negotiating?" his father said.

"Dad, it's exactly what I saw you do at yard sales."

———————

Paul started out with the title "director of Intuit small business Internet," which meant he was in charge of packaging Intuit's most lucrative product into a website—its small-business accounting software, called QuickBooks. A year or so later, he was knighted vice president of technology and product development, a role that obliged him to travel regularly between New England and California.

He maintained an odd suburban father's normalcy. He insisted on driving his daughter to school. Afterward, on a number of occasions, he'd drive to Logan airport, catch a midmorning plane to California, attend an afternoon's worth of meetings at Intuit headquarters in Mountain View, and fly back to Boston on a red-eye, arriving in time the next morning to drive his daughter to school again.

He could take naps on the plane if he felt like napping, or snooze in the waiting areas of airports, but not if he ran into someone he thought was worth recruiting. He had asked Karl to automate his email so that every message ended "Intuit is hiring in Boston!" Paul was always recruiting, everywhere he went, talking in rapid-fire hyperbole to every possible candidate. Software companies were always on the lookout for talent, but recruiting seemed to fill a need in Paul—for family improvement, he believed. After a while, when he arrived at Intuit headquarters, someone was bound to ask him, "Who'd you hire on the airplane today?"

He was moving fast. He worked long hours on Intuit business and also made time for projects on the side. He was financing a website for rating businesses, which he called Mancala. He was helping his brother Ed get a new company up and running—Intermute, which would develop antispam products. And he was trying to do something with the Worldwide Xiangqi League.

For a time, Paul paid a programmer to manage the Xiangqi site, but he liked the young man so much that he poached him from himself and sent him to work for Ed at Intermute. He did much the same thing at Intuit, sending the 10X coder Jeff Rago to Intuit's California headquarters, in order to "infect the culture there." Several times he asked Karl if he would take over the maintenance of the Xiangqi system. Karl told him, "I don't think so. Not anymore."

Hypothetically, the Xiangqi site could have kept on running by itself. But like gardens, websites die if left untended. All sorts of things can go wrong. Changes in technology can cause glitches in the system. Even a temporary power outage at a data center can bring down a site for good, if no one stands ready to reboot the software properly. Paul wrote Karl asking how many people were still playing at Club Xiangqi. "Oh, ten to twenty," Karl wrote back. When Karl looked again, a few years later, the imaginary palace had disappeared. It had died the little death of software. Karl didn't feel particularly nostalgic about it. For one thing, he had never played the game. Later he wrote that there were plenty of ghosts haunting the Web. He added this epitaph: "mice eating the last copy of a book in a library, a cuneiform tablet sinking into the Nile . . ."

Karl stayed on with Paul's Intuit team, taking care of the server computers that lay behind QuickBooks online, and working on special jobs for Paul, usually the automation of some dull administrative task.

After taxes, Karl's share from the sale of Boston Light amounted to about three million dollars. Paul urged him to invest some of his winnings in his start-up Mancala. Karl thought, *Who am I to say no?* That company failed, a fact Paul brought up for years afterward, in the spirit of a monk studying a skull. Paul lost two million dollars. Karl lost a hundred thousand. But then, not long afterward, Paul told Karl he should invest another hundred thousand in Intermute, and when that company was sold, Karl's investment turned into a million. He was amazed and a little dismayed. He told the accountant he shared with Paul, "There's something wrong here. I didn't do anything. I wrote a check. This system is not sustainable."

"That's capitalism," the accountant replied.

For a few early spring months, Karl lived in Paul's summer house in Hull. Karl and his girlfriend of fourteen years had broken up, and Paul told him to use the house on the ocean as if it were his own. Karl bought Paul a new piano to thank him for the stock in Boston Light—and for everything else. Karl had also begun to give away a large part of his winnings to help the family of a newfound friend, a woman he had encountered on the Internet. In December 1999, he and Paul exchanged these emails:

> karl: I have news: I've unexpectedly met the love of my life and am moving to Oregon early next year . . . Do you still want to employ me?
> pme: You're kidding.
> That's amazing.
> I'm dying to hear the details.
> Yes, I want you to work for us no matter where you are!
> Ok?

Two days later, Paul wrote again, on the same subject:

> pme: I've been thinking a *lot* about your situation over the past week.
> I have a lot of different emotions about your life right now, e.g.,

—I'm jumping for joy about your new love, and your optimism about it. :-)

—I'm very sad to have you leave Boston, for lots of different reasons. You are one of my closest friends, my family loves you, and especially over the past two years, you have become an important part of my own self identity. I'm scared to have you leave. :)

(I'm of course *not* suggesting you not leave, but I'm just telling you about my sadness.)

—To be honest, I'm a little scared with your reckless abandon with your newfound wealth. :(E.g., I'd like to manage $1MM of your BLS earnings for you :) so I can both help it grow and protect it from you. :)

Paul needn't have worried.

karl [many years later]: I kept plenty, enough so I wouldn't have to work again barring catastrophe (in which case we'll probably all starve to death anyway, so who cares) . . . At some pretty early point in the millions, except for people who use money to keep score (if any such actually exist in real life, I'm not sure), it's just a number.

By the time he wrote this, Karl had been living for a decade in a house on a remote shore of the Pacific, reading and listening to music and writing free software. He was also a leader of the group that maintained Knuth's TEX—an "exquisitely-cut diamond" thirty years old by then, an antique that had to be made to fit a constantly changing setting. Karl worked on these projects gratis, aware of the irony that work he had done on commercial software was paying his way.

9

THE BITTER END OF THE DOT-COM BUBBLE CAME IN THE MIDDLE of 2001, when the NASDAQ index reached its nadir, falling from around 5,000 at its height to around 1,100, a decline of about 78 percent in the value of the listed stocks. Paul's timing had been, as he put it, *"obscenely* lucky."

Of the Internet companies spawned in the era, more than half failed—many because they could no longer find investors to finance their losses after stock prices crashed. This might well have been the fate of Boston Light. But Paul just happened to sell near the top of the market, and when the crash came, he and his team were safely in the harbor of Intuit.

Paul's greatest luck, his purest, in which he had no hand at all, came on September 11, 2001. He and some colleagues had booked the doomed flight from Boston to Los Angeles, but at the last minute they switched to a less expensive itinerary. Paul was sitting on the cheaper flight, the plane still on the ground at Logan airport, when his wife called in tears and told him the news. Paul stood up and said to the cabin in general, "This plane's not going anywhere." Then he walked off, probably the last time one could exit an airplane without permission. He stopped to watch TV at an airport bar just long enough to see the video of the airplanes crashing into the World Trade Center. Then he drove home. It was hard to stop wondering about the stranger who might have taken his seat on the plane. He rarely told the story to anyone outside his family.

Paul left Intuit after only three and a half years. The company had paid him well in cash and stock, and he still had most of his money from the sale of Boston Light. He could afford not to work for a while, and he had a compelling reason. His father was suffering from Alzheimer's dementia, and, Paul told himself, he wanted to take care of him.

It was his mother's last wish that Paul do this. In the early spring of 2001, she gave Paul a journal that recorded his father's increasingly erratic behavior. Paul was astonished. His father's familiar gestures—rapping his knuckles on a table to emphasize a point, for instance—were all intact. But these were only camouflage, obscuring gathering dementia. The evidence was undeniable once Paul started looking for it.

His mother died three weeks later, and with a flourish. She asked that all her children gather in her room at New England Baptist Hospital. As always there were seven views of the scene, and also as usual, Paul's and his brother Tim's were the most nearly alike, and the darkest. Their father sat in a chair beside the bed where their mother lay propped up, her seven children ranged before her. To Paul and Tim, their father looked forlorn and confused, and the confusion was probably a blessing, if Paul's memory of his mother's speech was accurate: "I have felt for a long time that my marrying your father was a mistake, but looking at each of you, I see what you got from him, what you got from me, and only now I realize it was a success."

Then, according to Tim, she said, "Jesus is waiting for me, and this is my last day." She asked her children to say goodbye individually, and they went up one by one, in birth order, and hugged her.

Of the seven, Tim seemed to have, or at least was willing to express, the most objective feelings about his childhood. He said of his mother, "I wanted her to be my mommy, and there were too many kids to share her with." He also said, "Mom's lack of emotional warmth was hard. I always thought of her as cold, not mean-cold, detached. I kept looking for my mom to be warm, but I think I was near fifty before I figured out it wasn't going to happen." When his turn came, Tim went to her bedside and hugged her. He was crying. "Mom, Mom."

She didn't let this go on long. "Come on, now," she said. "There's others waiting."

Tim couldn't help but feel amused, her words expressed his problem so succinctly. "I could make a lot out of this," he told himself as he retreated.

When Paul's turn came, the next to last, he did as the others had done. He went to her bedside and gave her a hug. She didn't say goodbye, though. She gave him instructions. "Keep up the good work," she said. She added, "And take care of your father."

Paul was thirty-seven. He had earned a master's degree in computer science, he had been a senior vice president of three different software companies. He had created several enterprises of his own and sold one of them for millions. *Keep up the good work.* Most people would not have heard what Paul did in those familiar words. He thought his mother was saying he hadn't yet done enough to win her approval. Now he never would, but at least he could try to take care of his father.

There were bound to be difficult moments between a son and a fading father. Paul would take him out for short road trips, and every time the old man got settled in the passenger seat he would rediscover the navigation device, the GPS. He would stare at it and say to Paul, "What's that?" And Paul would explain, and his father would say, "Could *you* build one of those?" And Paul would say yes, and his father would smile. It gave Paul a wonderful feeling to see that smile. But then one day he took his father out in a different car. "Where's your other car?" Paul's father asked.

"In the shop," Paul said. "It needed a brake job."

"You're too good to do your own brakes now?" his father said.

His dad's scorn was unmistakable. Paul wanted to lift his chin and say, "I could do my own brakes. I *choose* to do other things." But it was far too late by then for Paul to declare himself, to say that he wasn't the same as everyone and didn't want to be.

Take care of your father. It became the hardest job Paul had ever known. He had a lot of help from his siblings and especially his sister Nancy, but his father's condition claimed more and more of his time. And more and more, "caregiving" seemed like another name for defeat.

One day he took his father out to lunch at the usual place, Bertucci's, in West Roxbury. At the table, his father kept saying the same things over and over. This was nothing new. Maybe that was the problem. Paul began to imagine others listening in. He felt embarrassed— for his father, by his father—and ashamed for feeling that way. He ordered a drink. He felt better, looser inside. Lunch over, he helped his father out to the car and clipped the seatbelt around him. Paul had begun backing up when someone in a car behind them leaned on his horn. Paul threw open his door and strode back to the honking car. He could see that the driver was a big guy, and he was glad. After a brief conversation—"What the fuck are you honking about?" "Fuck you, asshole!"—Paul grabbed the door handle. He was going to pull the guy out and get him on the ground, but during one of those lucid moments in the midst of madness Paul saw revelation cross the man's face—*This guy is nuts!*—and before Paul could get the door open, the man had locked it and rolled up his window. Then, from behind the glass, he resumed yelling threats.

Paul's hands were still trembling when he got back into his car. Then he saw his father's frightened face and heard the old man saying, almost in singsong, "Paul, be careful. Paul, be careful."

He read medical journals, researching his father's many illnesses—pituitary tumors and bladder cancer and late-onset diabetes and Alzheimer's dementia and the consequences of quadruple bypass surgery. He had long consultations with half a dozen specialists. His father was on twenty different medications when Paul got involved. He gradually reduced that number to eight. When necessary, he put diapers on his father.

Finally, Paul and his siblings agreed to put him in a nursing home. When his father took a fall there and hit his head and never woke up, Paul felt he'd killed him. He was an engineer, after all. He knew about the connectedness of things. If he had studied his father's condition more diligently, he would have realized that Alzheimer's robs its victims of their motor skills, that his father was at risk for falling, and that special steps had to be taken to keep him safe. Paul looked for ways to excuse himself. He had been worn-out, he hadn't hired enough help. But his mind was unconvinced. *I failed. My mom told me to take care of him, and I failed.*

Paul descended into what he called "a dark place," that familiar region of sleepless nights and nameless fear, of sitting by windows waiting for dawn. His marriage came undone. This was something he seldom talked about to anyone, though he would say he felt the fault was his. It was a source of lingering guilt. He moved out—his choice—and lived for a time that winter in the summer house in Hull. Joe Mahoney was still advising Intuit. Paul would meet him periodically for breakfast or drinks in Cambridge. "I just have a lot of anger issues," Mahoney remembered Paul telling him. Paul would say, "I tend to anger, and I just don't deal with it very well." Sometimes, at 4 A.M., Mahoney would awake to the ringing of his phone and hear Paul speaking to him half coherently. Mahoney was usually too groggy to make much sense of what Paul said, but the tenor of Paul's voice was unmistakable. "Total panic attack," Mahoney called it.

In his office at home, Paul kept a photograph of the psychiatrist he shared with Tom White. In the picture, the doctor—Jack Green—is a small man with liver spots on the backs of his hands, deep-creased cheeks and forehead, a ropy neck, salt-and-pepper hair, and he wears a comforting smile. One's eye is drawn to the array of things around him: trays full of papers, bookcases filled with books and looseleaf binders, photographs, containers holding items such as greeting cards and scribbled notes, a box of staples, a jar of pens, a few pill bottles. For all its clutter, the corner of the doctor's office seems not orderly, but not random, either. One imagines that the things around him are arrayed in odd, complex streams of association, like the memories within a mind that has taken in a lot and has sorted it out well enough for periodic use, like a rendering of what Proust calls "the vast structure of recollection."

Paul first went to see him shortly after his father died. Dr. Green was in his early eighties then. He had a calmness about life and its vicissitudes that made his advice convincing. "Whatever your crisis is, stop and take a breath. Because nothing has to be addressed today," Dr. Green would tell him, and Paul would feel calmer at once. Paul began visiting him every week. He wouldn't let Paul pay. "These sessions are so interesting I should pay *you*," he said.

Dr. Green hadn't kept up on the new crops of psychoactive drugs, but he felt Paul should probably try some of them. So he sent Paul to the chief psychiatrist at Mass General, and with his help Paul began what was to be a long search for antidotes, other than lithium, to bipolar disorder.

In the first years of this quest, Paul tried and quit about a dozen medications. Two made him so groggy that he didn't dare to drive. One made the roof of his mouth crack from dryness, another gave him irritable bowel syndrome, still another made his hands tremble so violently he couldn't hold on to a cup of tea. Except for the drugs that had sedated him, none dampened his highs. He did have the one great success, the antiepileptic drug Lamictal that had eliminated almost all his episodes of depression. Neurological tests indicated that Paul had temporal lobe epilepsy—the most common form of partial epilepsy and, he was told, the probable cause of the gigantic clocks and doors and other visual distortions that he had first experienced as a child. Those also mostly ceased once he started taking the antiepileptic.

Hypomania, however, still came and went. Had it helped him in his role of entrepreneur, boosting his energy and boldness? Or had he made his way in spite of hypomania?

In Paul's telling, the Kayak creation story began with Tom White. He had long urged Paul to go to Haiti. In need of a new purpose after his father's death, Paul finally obliged him. He visited the hospital built by Partners In Health largely with Tom's money, and came back shaken, with images of the worst of Haiti burned into his memory—children behind barriers at the airport who looked as if they were starving, dressed in rags and begging; ruined roads and dirt-floored huts all along the way to the hospital, where patients lay on the verge of death from illnesses long since banished from the United States. He returned with a new project in mind, which he remembered expressing this way, with his usual earnest exaggeration, to a venture capitalist over the phone: "I want to get back. I have been not working for a year because I was taking care of my dad. I want to get back and create a company again, and I want to make an obscene amount of money so I can do the right thing and help Haiti."

The venture capitalist invited Paul to be an EIR, entrepreneur in residence, at his firm, Greylock. Paul and his old sidekick Jim Giza took up residence in an office there, and then one day Paul got a call from his former boss at Interleaf, Larry Bohn. He was working for another venture firm, General Catalyst, in Cambridge. Bohn asked Paul if he'd drop by and evaluate an investment the firm was considering. And while Paul was there, he was introduced to Steve Hafner, a young man who had helped to found the online travel company Orbitz. Hafner had been collaborating with General Catalyst on an idea for something different, and lucrative. He and Paul went to lunch, at the Legal Sea Foods restaurant just an elevator ride down from General Catalyst.

Paul told this story many times in the coming years—privately to friends and publicly to students. Sometimes he emphasized all the luck involved, how accidental it had been for him to meet Steve Hafner. Sometimes he emphasized the persuasiveness of Hafner's pitch: That travel was 8 percent of the entire U.S. economy and the largest segment of e-commerce. That there was an empty space waiting for a company that didn't sell anything to the user but conducted truly comprehensive travel searches, making its money on referral fees and ads. General Catalyst had already pledged five million. Paul agreed to join up as Steve's equal partner.

Sometimes Paul recited the details with a swagger. Many would have done the same. Kayak was one of those success stories that encouraged bravado. And maybe Paul's telling was also colored by a touch of hypomania, a rising sense of mastery, also present in the event itself: "And then Steve and I went downstairs to Legal Sea Foods and had a couple drinks. He gave me the pitch, I gave him feedback, and we talked about the travel industry. And then he said he was looking for a CTO, and I said, 'I'll find you one, what are you paying?' And he said, 'A buck fifty and four percent.' I said, 'That sounds great. It's a good space.' I said, 'I run a mailing list in Boston called Boston CTOs. It's the best tech guys in Boston.' I go, 'I'll find someone for you.' And Steve said, 'Why don't *you* do it?' And I said, 'No, no, I want to start another company again. I sold my last one to Intuit, and I have an office at Greylock.' And he said, 'What would it take to have you do it?' And I said, 'Well, at a minimum, it's fifty-fifty.' And he said, 'Done.'"

Hafner extended his hand across the table. He was about Paul's age, a handsome fellow but in an entirely different way from Paul, thinner and smaller and impeccably groomed—a tailored jacket, manicured nails. Paul wore jeans, and hadn't bothered to shave that day. He didn't usually drink at lunch, the way his father had. He tended to use alcohol less for pleasure than for tamping down the speed of his thoughts, the ballooning of elation. But at least in retrospect, gin did nothing to dampen his spirits that day. He was pleased with himself. Hafner was clearly a big shot. Demanding half of the new company from him was brash. Paul reached across the table and shook Hafner's proffered hand. There was one last item. Hafner said he was putting a million dollars of his own into this venture. Paul said okay, he'd put in a million, too.

This was hardly a unique transaction: two guys investing some of their own money in their start-up. There was even a cliché for it—having skin in the game. On the other hand, they had only just met. Hafner liked the sound of Paul's account of his exploits in the software business, but he didn't bother to check it out. Moreover, a million dollars was about a third of Hafner's net worth and still a lot of money to Paul, who had an ex-wife and children to support. And for all of that, the entire transaction took only forty-five minutes.

Describing the moment in one of his talks to young would-be entrepreneurs, Paul said that he and Hafner were confident to the point of *arrogance*, daring to the point of *recklessness*. Certainly their deal qualified as risky. But after they made it, they proceeded more prudently than many founders did: paid attention to both sides of their balance sheet, kept expenses low, realized a profit within a year and a half, and never lost money after that. Paul often said he felt like a daredevil when he was making his deal with Hafner. He must have calmed down quickly, because an hour or so afterward, he called Billo. Then he called Schwenk.

PART IV

APPS

1

SPY POND WAS COVERED WITH SNOW. IT WAS MIDWINTER 2013. The sale of Kayak wouldn't close until late spring, and for now Paul remained its CTO. Blade, the new company, the incubator that he wanted to start, was still in the dream stage. But in his mind, he was already moving on.

On a morning at the end of February, Paul woke up in the dark feeling nauseated but with a vivid picture of Blade's office in his mind. He hadn't found the actual place yet, but he had seen it in greater detail than before. He jotted down notes, then got up and typed a list. There was "Furniture," including two styles of chairs, "tons of easily accessible power outlets and cat5 jacks," and "whiteboards everywhere." There were "Drinks": an espresso machine, a "wall of healthy snacks" to be stored in "awesome glass containers or OXO pop-ups," and no unhealthy beverages, with the possible exception of Grey Goose vodka. "Entertainment" included many amplifiers, "lots of speakers," "cool color-changing lights." And under "Maybe/Not Yet": "treadmill, sleep place, foosball, pool table, darts, etc."

In one of his early morning routines, Paul would write up his ideas of the night and afterward he would meditate—he had set up a room for the purpose adjacent to his bedroom. Then he would get showered and dressed and breakfasted, and finally he would lug his computer to his dining room table and answer email for a while, squeezing in a few more minutes of work before heading off into a day packed with appointments. But this morning was different. This morning, after he wrote up his Blade office document, there was nothing at hand absorbing enough to distract him from his nausea.

Sunrise found him lying on his living room couch. In the tall windows beside him, across Spy Pond, the rush hour traffic on Route 2 moved in fits and starts, red lights dotting the gray winter's dawn, the cars' horns silenced by distance and glass. Paul lay stretched out on his back, in coffin position and pallid light, his hair combed, his chin up, his hands folded on his stomach. "I started a new drug last night," he said. He stared at the ceiling, his face composed. Evidently he was trying to confront his nausea—an effort in mindfulness perhaps, in trying to separate nausea from himself, to turn nausea into an object and put it back inside the pill that had caused it.

Hypomania had been stirring, he explained. He hadn't been sleeping much, and he had been feeling "very reckless." His psychiatrist had urged him to try a new antimania drug.

"It's amazing that such a tiny pill can make you so sick," Paul said toward the ceiling. "Five milligrams." The choice was familiar. He'd already made it. No way he was going to take that little pill again.

In early March, Paul found the site for Blade's office, the basement of a building on Fort Point Channel, across from downtown Boston: a half-underground, concrete-floored and completely unadorned four-

thousand-square-foot chamber, once a Chinese restaurant but unten-
anted for twenty years, with a row of windows facing the water. When
his realtor took him there, Paul peered in the grimy windows, and he felt
as though he had seen the place already, maybe in a dream. "It's gritty
and edgy and on the water," he told his realtor. "Let's do it."

Billo and Schwenk were as good as signed up, and his favorite
two-man UI-building team had said they might also leave Kayak and
follow him. Paul wasn't very secretive about his designs, and on a day
in late March Steve Hafner arrived without warning in Concord. In
the privacy of a conference room, he asked Paul if the rumors were
true. Was Paul poaching members of his team? Paul said he was, and
Hafner said, "*Dude*, have you *read* your employment contract?"

Paul had, of course, but not for years. He'd often done things
this way: negotiate deals "ferociously," then forget about the details
and move on. He had forgotten that his Kayak contract contained
provisions against enticing employees to follow him to another company, especially those who reported directly to him, such as Billo and
Schwenk. Paul didn't feel any better when he realized he had made
many of his overtures in emails—as a legal matter, virtually in public.

Paul was already in violation of his contract, Hafner pointed out.
Shortly afterward, Paul headed for downtown Boston to negotiate
the lease for Blade's office. "Steve just doesn't want me to have more
fun than he does," he said as he drove. "It's all bullshit. I love a fight.
I want to resolve everything peacefully, but I do love a fight. It's kind
of like fear. It's exciting." He muttered, speaking of Steve: "He has
to be careful. Don't corner a tiger." By the next day Paul felt almost
contrite. He must have scared Steve by moving so fast on Blade, he
figured. Steve planned to stay on at Kayak, but clearly he'd been arguing for both of their interests: to protect Paul from a lawsuit and
the still-pending sale of Kayak, as well as to protect the company's
future. This was something Paul cared about, too. "I do *not* want

Kayak to fail," he said. Steve had visited Concord on a Friday. On Sunday, Paul wrote, "My mood was interesting this weekend. On Friday afternoon, I felt kind of bummed about Steve's comments to me. But Saturday morning I was filled with energy, and excited about change of any type."

Paul put Blade on hold for a while and turned his fervor to the American Gun League, the AGL, redoubling his efforts to make it real. He read about guns and gun control, on all sides of the issue. He arranged meetings and phone calls, seeking advice—not always but often listening hard, touching his upper lip with an index finger as if to make sure the lip stayed put: Don't worry about assault rifles; concentrate on the mayhem caused by stolen guns and on the twenty thousand Americans who shot themselves to death each year.

He flew repeatedly to New York and Washington and once to California, looking for advice and donors. He wasn't having much luck assembling a board of directors, but he kept on describing his ideal group: "When they're on a stage, my guys will be so strong the NRA will wet their pants." When he found an executive director— a former Marine colonel who had served with great distinction, including in combat—Paul began describing him this way: "He's a thirty-four-year Marine vet, he led four thousand troops into southern Iraq, he collects art, he can talk about eighteenth-century French literature, and he could take out this whole restaurant in eleven seconds." On one occasion, a person who had met the colonel listened to this litany and then remarked, in all innocence, that he hadn't realized the colonel read French, and Paul nudged the questioner with an elbow and smiled.

He put up his own money to get the AGL started, about a quarter of a million dollars in all, for the domain names and logo and website designs, and later for salaries and the rent on an AGL office.

His agenda was still an association of gun owners who wanted "common sense laws for gun safety." But it is hard to raise enthusiasm, let alone money, on behalf of moderation. He sought out wealthy gun-owning Republicans. Evidently they disliked the NRA's fanaticism, but they weren't apt to suffer from it. Paul hadn't yet found anyone who would match the half million more that he was willing to give.

Road Wars was still in progress. Five years before, Paul had nearly lost his license because of speeding tickets. This was not an option for the divorced father of two kids, he'd reasoned. So he'd sold all his fast cars. "And I bought a fucking Subaru station wagon with a small engine. It was my rehab car." He got no tickets for a couple of years and gradually began rebuilding his fleet. The latest addition was an all-electric Tesla. He was in such a hurry to get the car's cosmetics right that he drove it to a customizing shop in a spring snowstorm, the rear-wheel-drive high-torque car slipping and sliding like a toboggan on the roads. He brought it home decked out like his other cars—black all over, debadged, dechromed. Whichever car he chose in the morning was a venue for Road Wars, the app playing on his iPhone mounted on the dash. He'd been averaging two moving violations a year since his rehabilitation. But since he'd started playing the test versions of the game, he had been stopped only once and given a warning—by a cop who turned out to have a lot of questions about Paul's Audi R8.

Paul figured Road Wars would probably never make money: "Ninety-nine percent of games fail. So I'm prepared." Still, he spent some hours every week discussing refinements with the friends he paid to program the app, and clearly this was worth all the time and expense to him. "I just lost six coin for driving too fast," he said one day at the wheel as the app on his dashboard blinked blazing red and emitted the sound of crashing metal and glass. "Being a competitive person, I have to drive safer," he said, slowing down. Then he added, with exultation in his voice: "This is having *exactly* the effect on me that I intended it to have on kids."

He opened the windows of his living room to greet and photograph the first March snow falling on Spy Pond. "I'm excited about this storm. I didn't think we were getting any more snow, so it's kind of nice to have one more." Three weeks later he greeted the next snowstorm in the same spirit. "Every time people bitch about the new snow I just get delighted. I know it's not going to last for long. I just think it's really pretty."

2

PAUL'S PLACE BY THE POND HAD A CURIOUS HISTORY. THE LAND AND the oldest section of his house were once part of the estate of a nineteenth-century magnate named Addison Gage, an entrepreneur of ice. He harvested it from Spy Pond and other locales and shipped it far and wide, to America's warm southern states and also, according to one local chronicle, "to the East and West Indies, to China, to India, to South America, even to Australia." Paul knew some of the history and would entertain guests with it, drawing a moral: No matter how wacky, an idea can succeed if it aims at a big market (all those hot places without refrigeration) and if there are technologies to execute it (special saws, sawdust in the holds of sailing ships, insulated buildings).

What vision the ice barons of New England must have had, to look at the ice on a Spy Pond and think, *I could send this to India.* It was a fitting heritage for Paul.

For years, ideas for new enterprises had flowed into his mind, usually at night. He would attach names to the relative few that survived the morning. Karl used to register these as Internet domains, and Paul would put them on a master list. In 2013, it contained 158 names. Karl had never known what some of them signified. Paul himself had forgotten some: APPMOVE, CARDBLOCK, CLOAKLY, GOANDCO, PAYTONES, SEARCHLETS, SOFTWARESURVEY, TOWER51. Likewise DRAGINBOX. He gazed at it. "I don't remember. But it was something really fucking cool."

Some names denoted nothing. He just liked their sound: AVIDFOX, CONNEXAS, CONNEXOS, ENIGENCE, ETELL, HEROPORT, SYNVEO. Some unattached names came from trips—ZARZAN from Norway, UMANU and TUMTUM from Kenya. Some he'd found by brainstorming through the alphabet. Once, years back, he wrote a short piece of code, a software robot that would find every two-character domain that was still unregistered. The script produced fifty names—such as "Bl"—but he bought only a few, and still counted this among his important commercial mistakes. By now, he figured, every two-letter combination had probably been claimed, and each was probably worth at least $100,000. He and Steve Hafner had spent $30,000 on KAYAK.COM back in 2004. This had soon looked like a bargain, because they had failed to also buy the German domain name KAYAK.DE, and a few years later they ended up paying 100,000 euros for it.

Technically, you can't buy a domain name, but you can in essence rent the exclusive use of one. In the early days of the Web, you almost always did this through an official registry, and you could claim most names for a nominal price. But now, in 2013, about 270 million domains had been registered. Traffic in names had become like a vast international used car business, where the rights to names were bought and sold, some for astonishing prices—typically, brand names or descriptive names likely to turn up early in a Web search ($30.6 million for INSURANCE.COM was the current record). Paul made a hobby of playing around in this market, a yard sale haunted by crafty middlemen and shady characters. Just recently, he'd spent $26,000 on two dot-com domains—$10,000 for the initials of his gun control venture, AGL, and $16,000 for ROADWARS. To recover some of his trading capital, he had recently sold SNAPCAB for $10,000. The idea behind that name was a mobile-app-based system of taxis and limousines. It approximated—and predated by about five years—the basic plan of Uber, a current e-commerce phenomenon whose value was placed in the billions. Paul had wanted to build SNAPCAB for Kayak, but Hafner had discouraged him—wary, not without cause, of Paul's distractibility.

Prescience is a retrospective virtue. Paul's way of saying this was to tell how he had been introduced to the people who were starting YouTube and had thought, *Yeah. Whatever.* The company on which he had lost two million, Mancala, was a version of the now profitable websites dispensing advice to consumers, a Yelp precursor, a good idea pursued too early, an example of premature prescience. SNAPCAB had been prescience unpursued, a might-have-been. Paul's list of names contained a couple more of those: BOSTONBOUNCE, which, like Groupon, would have sold discounted coupons to consumers; ERADIO, which might have been an early satellite radio company. His list contained a passel of stillborn software talent agencies that would have served both domestic and foreign markets. These ranged from BOSTONASSIST to MUMBAICODERS. A few names of this species memorialized dreams of stirring up economic development in African countries where he had philanthropic interests: KENYACODERS, NAIROBICODERS, KIGALICODERS.

Of these, only KIGALICODERS had come to life, just briefly, in Rwanda. "We found some kids in Kigali. We wanted to teach them to be coders so they could make some money. We built a simple website. We taught them how to bid on jobs on Rentacoder. The company failed, and I don't know why."

Some names were souvenirs: XIANGQI.COM, BOSTONLIGHT.COM, which he had bought back from Intuit. F7 was the chorded command that used to summon up his email program and now recalled the decade when he and Karl had emailed each other at least once a day. PARKINGPATH recalled the blinding light of a hypomanic hour when he was listening to an urban architect talk on public radio about the importance of trees, and suddenly realized that he must start a campaign—no, a movement—to bring tree-shaded paths to parking lots, one for every two hundred cars.

There was GOODENOUGHSOFTWARE, a nod to the way his father had of pounding in a nail and saying, "That's good enough." The idea sprang from irritation: "Microsoft keeps releasing a new version of Office every year. Who needs all those bullshit features? I would take the ten most successful software apps and strip them down to the twenty percent most people use." There was SIMPLELIST, a design for the simplest way to make a list. And KWHEEL, a tool for counting the numbers of colors on websites. MAILSTATS came from a program that Karl wrote for him back in Interleaf days; it let your employees analyze their email usage and gave them tips on how to curb the excess. There were BUZZCARZ, a now defunct discussion forum about cars; BOSTONDETAIL, a mobile service for cleaning cars; and CARSICK, an app to resolve arguments between husbands and wives as to who was the better driver, which, along with PRODRIVEAPP and WHIPWARS (in current teen talk, "whips" meant cars), had led on to Road Wars, its future still in doubt.

SECRETINSIDETHEORANGE was the name of a movie he planned to make, in order to introduce xiangqi to the Western world. The name comes from an ancient Chinese fable: Two very large oranges are found in an orchard and cut open to reveal, in each, two very small and elderly men intently playing xiangqi. Traditionally, only boys had been taught the game, so he planned to have a young Chinese woman explain the rules on camera. He had long since made an outline of a script and still told himself he'd make the film next year.

Of civic projects that had died or never been tried out, there were CENTRALAUTHORITY (to identify and debunk, through parody, lies gone viral on the Web) and KIDMAIL (to protect children from online pornography and predators): "I didn't pursue it enough."

PURPLEWATCH was a favorite. "I want to be judgmental about people who buy $10,000 watches, but you're talking to a guy who buys $200,000 cars." He would execute the plan when he found the time: He gets Swatch to make an inexpensive all-purple watch. They sell it for $10,000. The profit goes to a charitable foundation. The people who buy the watches get to say where the foundation sends their ten thousand, and they also get to show off their luridly colored watches to people at their country clubs and to say, as Paul would have it: "I'm rich, too, motherfucker. Except my ten grand went to an orphanage."

In the realm of ideas, regret was a waste of time. Better to think of the handful of successes. IVRCHEATSHEET.COM referred to the interactive voice response systems used by every big corporation. The idea had come to him around 2002, in the days when his father was slipping into dementia and Paul began hearing him try to talk to the robotic voices at Comcast and Verizon. "And I'm like, Okay, I took his car away. Now these machines are taking his phone and TV away. I might as well dig a hole in my backyard and stick him in it. So I was like, The guy should be able to talk to humans. He's paying these assholes at Comcast a hundred dollars a month. Why won't they talk to him?"

Paul raised this question on PAULENGLISH.COM. He asked readers to send him the unpublicized numbers and codes that would con-

nect to the phones of actual people at big companies—numbers that
would circumvent the offensive, indeed "evil," IVRs. Paul posted the
numbers on his blog. Word spread. Phone numbers poured in. The
Globe did a story about the local software entrepreneur who was taking on the giants of corporate America. *People* magazine and *The
New York Times* ran articles. Paul appeared on NPR and the BBC
and national television shows, and his blog went viral—a million visitors in just one month. So he created the website. His assistant at
Kayak told him he needed a better name for it. She came up with
GETHUMAN. Karl, out in Oregon, secured the new name, and Paul
created the site. It contained a list of the various secret numbers and
codes and procedures that would connect you to a human being at
a company—four hundred companies and growing when the *Times*
article appeared—and advice on how to use those numbers, and also
Paul's thoughts about how companies ought to treat their customers.
He told the *Times* reporter he wanted GetHuman to lead a movement that would "change the face of customer service."

In one of his lectures to students, Paul said: "A lot of successful companies' products are created not with a business plan but instead from how much the person is irritated. And those people just
say, I don't care, or This makes me so angry I'm going to dedicate a
year to doing this, and then if the product is really good and people
start using it, then they figure out how they can make money on it."
GetHuman had accomplished the first part of that sequence. It had
gained a large audience, and large audiences can sometimes be mon-
etized. But Kayak was only two years old. Paul didn't have time to figure out how to make money with another website, let alone carry on a
movement. Eventually he handed GetHuman to a young coder friend,
who made it into a small but profitable company. Traffic to its site was
still growing, on its way toward fifty million different visitors a year.

BUZZMED had turned into a website called Global Health Delivery, GHDONLINE.ORG—a flourishing online branch of a system created by Partners In Health and Brigham and Women's Hospital. The idea was to codify and disseminate proven techniques for fixing things like public water supplies in impoverished places and for treating illnesses such as tuberculosis and malaria. For about a year, Paul had stretched his working hours, running Kayak engineering while designing the online forum and assembling a team to build it.

JOINAFRICA would have extended that work, spreading the Internet all over the continent. An overly enthusiastic public performance ended with a magazine story headlined "Kayak.com Cofounder Paul English Plans to Blanket Africa in Free Wireless Internet." Paul thought this made him sound racist, a great white bwana who would wire all of Africa: "I had two weeks of near panic attacks." But he did bring Internet access to medical outposts in Burundi, Uganda, Zambia, and Malawi, buying the satellite dishes and other equipment, hiring others to install them, and sometimes traveling to the sites himself to help.

It was a consultant who had come up with KAYAK. An imperfect name, Paul told students when lecturing on "branding," because most Americans probably didn't know how to spell it. He remembered the day when that issue became moot, when he learned that merely typing "K" into Google brought up Kayak as the first option. "We own a letter!" he had shouted to his team. An odd name for a travel company, a kayak being one of the slowest forms of travel known, but the marketing consultant had pointed out that the palindromic Ks were memorable, and a kayak was, as she put it, "a vessel that allows an individual to easily navigate turbulent waters." You might see the name and subconsciously imagine that even your airplane ride would be scenic, quiet, healthful.

BLADE was his favorite name, also one of his oldest, registered by Karl on November 22, 1998. Paul had applied it to several enterprises, most recently the little group working on Road Wars. But he had always felt that BLADE was meant for something big. It fit most of his criteria for excellence in an online business name: short (no more than three syllables long), easy to spell, discernible even if spoken over a cellphone with a bad connection. And it had the advantage that outside of cutlery it didn't really denote anything, and could therefore be applied to almost any kind of enterprise and make it sound shiny, up-to-date, maybe a little dangerous.

In his mind the new Blade was looking more and more like a potpourri. It would provide "foster care" to "baby start-ups," all based on "big ideas." QSHOP, from the days of Boston Light, might assemble online the inventories and branding power of ten of America's most popular retailers and do battle with the likes of Amazon.com. Maybe another Blade company would create an online bank to rival the giant Fidelity. He hadn't named that concept yet. For the moment he called it "a Fidelity-killer."

Kayak, his big score, had been built on an idea that came from other people. There was no shame in this for him. As he would say, ideas are cheap, and worthless without execution. Yet ideas kept coming, as if Paul were channeling the ice baron as he slept in his house beside Spy Pond. The mind, after all, is an incubator. Blade was meant to be a dreamer of dreams, an idea of ideas, Paul's mind made incarnate.

3

JACK GREEN HAD DIED TEN YEARS AGO, AND PAUL HAD BEEN LOOK-
ing for a replacement ever since. His search continued as, on one
spring morning, he pulled up in front of a house on a quiet residential street. There were buds on the trees. He got out and smiled
toward the house of his latest psychologist. "All right. I'll be all fixed
in an hour."

Now it was May, and the grass that sloped down to Spy Pond was
green and growing, and the geese were back and shitting on it. When
he'd moved into his house, Paul had told his neighbors he would
put a stop to this, and they had smiled knowingly, and he'd set out
to show them: fox urine sprayed on the grass, a light that came on
automatically after sunset and mimicked a fox's eyes, a device that
broadcast the calls of hawks. Maybe this summer those interventions
would work.

Change was in the air. In the third week of May, Kayak's sale became official at last. Stock options could be cashed in. Schwenk had
stopped coming to work two weeks before. Paul had asked him to do

this, figuring that so long as Schwenk was around, everyone with a problem would keep asking him to fix it, and no one or no group of people would begin to learn his roles.

Billo waited until late May to depart. He announced his resignation in an email:

> Hey KAYAK,
> All good things must come to an end, and after over 3,400 days, 6,600 checkins, and 626,324 lines of code, so must our time together . . .
> KAYAK has been by far the most fun I've ever had at work, and you are the best team I've known. I hope you are all as proud as I am of what we made together, and I hope you continue to make it a little better every day . . .
> Love, Billo

On his final day, Billo gave a talk about the technical history of Kayak and told a few stories from the early days. Almost everyone in the Concord office attended, and when Billo was done, the engineering team stood and applauded, a rare event in the annals of an unsentimental trade.

As for Paul, he couldn't in good conscience yet say a formal goodbye. He had to coach a new CTO and oversee the transition.

––––––

Around the time the sale closed, Paul recorded a long weekend of internal turbulence—two days reminiscent of the nights when he lay on the floor waiting for dawn and then, on the third day, the opposite:

> I had an awful weekend home alone. And today I am super manic. My body is screaming with energy. Mind rushing. Hard to type.

I'm seeking help. And going to stop drinking at least for the week
until I stabilize.

He called his psychiatrist, who prescribed an antipsychotic called
Seroquel, used among other things for acute cases of depression and
mania. It was a drug Paul had tried and rejected a few years before
because it had left him feeling groggy for about two weeks. Following
the doctor's orders now, he took 50 milligrams. Soon afterward he
called his doctor and said, "I'm feeling weird." His doctor said, "Tri-
ple the dose." Paul slept for eighteen hours. He felt restored when he
woke up. He stopped taking the drug, and soon he was heading full
speed in several directions again. Blade was foremost.

"This summer I'm not even doing a financing plan for Blade,
I'm just designing a great office," he said. It was enough to keep him
busy. He had decisions to make about power and heat and bathroom
fixtures, about how to secure gigabit Internet access, still hard to
obtain in Boston. No detail was too small to be examined, not even
the Blade business card, even though he hadn't used one for years.
He had research to conduct at nightclubs, taking photos of features
he thought he might borrow. There were new neighbors to meet at
local art galleries and shows.

Fort Point, the site of Blade's incipient office, was an old industrial
neighborhood and for many years home to a community of artists
now at risk of being displaced by rising rents and law firms. A website
advertising loft rentals in Fort Point described it as a place where one
could "live inspired." You could walk through Blade's immediate pre-
cincts in perfect safety and find a bistro, but the old brick buildings
remained, with faded advertisements, the pentimento of commerce
past, painted on their walls. The flourishes around windows and cor-
nices suggested old-time masons with the freedom to invent. You
could wander down the oddly sloping sidewalk on Summer Street

on June evenings and imagine this was still an old and moody half-abandoned neighborhood.

The Blade office looked less inviting. It remained much as Paul had found it, a dank, dark concrete chamber like a dungeon, with tangles of pipes and wires in the ceiling. Paul went there nearly every day now, to confer with his architect and various contractors, and also to administer the Blade tour for invited guests—friends from the varied parts of his life, sound engineers, potential investors, fellow entrepreneurs. He would say he was trying to stir up interest, but the tours seemed like a source of pure pleasure for him, and any audience would do.

If guests came down the stairs from the building's front entrance, Paul would insist on leading them back outside so they could have the full experience. He'd take them out to the short alley that ran along one side of the building and, talking fast, he'd lead them to a somewhat battered green metal door.

So imagine that it's Blade-by-night and you are coming to one of my monthly, or maybe bimonthly, Blade events. You're walking down this sketchy-looking alley toward this funky green metal door where a six-foot-eight-inch Haitian bouncer stands guard. As you come inside, the lights begin to pulse, you open the black curtain that will be hanging here at the top of what will be a short flight of stairs, and suddenly you see your face and a sequence of your favorite photos all displayed on Blade's many screens, while the ubiquitous speakers play your favorite song.

Paul, in jeans and boots, smiling, takes his guests out onto the barren, dusty concrete floor, under the tangle of pipes and wires, and, still talking fast, describes the furnishings to come. *Thirty desks are spread across the open floor. Each desk rests on wheels, which are easily unlocked, and then the desks are rolled into a storage room that will be built over there, out back, so that in no time at all the office is transformed into a nightclub, which has a stage and DJ platform and a kick-ass sound and video system distributed among the four conference rooms* (named Fenway, Lizard, Toad, and Wally, in honor of the ballpark and three favorite clubs). *The place is insanely interactive, each desk containing integrated industrial power circuits. And there are sensors everywhere in here, and actuators opening and closing switches that control light, color, vibration, heat. And the interactive system connects wirelessly to the Blade wristbands, which friends and artists and technologists and some lucky investors will receive.*

Say it's Blade-by-day time, and the central software learns from the GPS on Billo's phone that Billo is half an hour away. Light strips on the floor beside his desk begin pulsing a light yellow. And if it's a nice day, mine will be blue, to say I'm taking my boat out, anyone want to come? (The boat was a thirty-foot motorboat with "the sickest sound system in Boston Harbor.")

Paul points to the far side of the chamber. Eyes by now adjusted to the half-light, a guest can make out an imposing wall made of huge, dark blocks of granite. Somewhere near it, the Blade bar will be constructed. *You'll see it from the doorway. In Blade-by-day it's hidden by pull-down screens. Montages of photos and videos are playing on them, the creations of local artists maybe, but really crazy artistic stuff. And then, in Blade-by-night, those screens roll up, and there's the bar. Behind it stands a* Maxim *magazine hottest-bartender-in-the-U.S. runner-up, already signed up for the job. Embedded in the bar there's a sensor, which looks like a hockey puck, with the Blade logo on its face. You place your Blade-banded hand on it and just like that, LEDs on the open shelves behind the bar light up your favorite beverages. So let's say your regular gin, Hendrick's, always lights up, but maybe you change your mind one night and you open the bar app on your phone and order a Dirty Black Russian, and when you get to the bar the LEDs will light*

up the Grey Goose vodka and the Kahlúa—and there might even be
some sort of indicator to signify the splash of Coke that goes on top.

The Blade tours came in great sustained mouthfuls, Paul eliding
words and phrases (as in "One interesting about it," with "thing" left
out). Each tour, it seemed, contained one or two new features, which
you imagined he had dreamed up in the night or maybe was inventing
as he spoke. The space was full of concrete columns, which couldn't
be removed—they held up the century-old building above. This was
a problem, but Paul had confronted it. "So what I'm gonna do is, I'm
going to have color-changing LED fixtures at the top of each face
of each column, so there'll be four fixtures each column, and they'll
be DMX-controlled, and so now the DJ can control the colors of the
columns. The columns are going to change to the music, and also we
can do things like, let's say in one sequence all the columns are pink,
but there's a woman in the club I would want to target, not target
but make the focus of the club. Because everyone has to wear an ID
tag in my club, I can say, 'Feature her,' so wherever she walks, the
columns turn red. So that's something you couldn't do if you didn't
have columns. So I'm taking something that's a weakness and turning it into a strength."

4

SOME OF PAUL'S FRIENDS TOLD HIM THEY DIDN'T THINK HE WAS bipolar. Sure, he could be impulsive and extravagant in many ways, but that was just a normal part of him, just Paul being Paul. Of course, he knew that what the doctors called hypomania was for him a different state from what those friends had witnessed. He could feel "the fire" spreading through his body as well as his mind. But from the outside, the difference between the exuberant and the hypomanic Paul wasn't always obvious. For one thing, hypomania in him was not a constant state. You could imagine he was in it, and then feel certain he was not. For another, he made efforts not to let the fire show. He tried to soften his grand gestures by openly poking fun at them, and when he said something that might conceivably have been taken as conceited—such as "I think that my name has some value" or "I'm kind of known as a recruiter"—he was apt to pin his hands between his knees and pull his shoulders inward, as if to make his body small. When he said the NRA wasn't going to know what hit them, that he was a tiger who shouldn't be cornered, that he was going to hire the best people in New York for Blade and *hunt down* Fidelity—was that just Paul working himself up for a challenge, employing versions of his big-number strategy, or was it Paul overtaken by the fire?

If you spent some time with him, you began to think that you could sense when his inner state had changed. You were aware that his natural charm had been eclipsed—the quietness that he could summon, his sense of the moment and of the needs of others in a room. Sometimes you could even feel in yourself a rising agitation, a hurried air. A respected neurologist and psychiatrist named Andres Kanner put the matter this way: "One of the things that any psychiatrist has discovered when in the company of a hypomanic person, they notice that the symptoms of hypomania are contagious."

Paul had long ago realized that hypomania was more exhilarating for him than for the people around him. "When I'm on fire, I only have ten seconds for a conversation, and I just blow by people," he once said. "Can I get away with it? I think most people like me, but I know I make mistakes." He could describe his bouts with the fire lucidly when it had abated, and once in a while even when it was taking hold of him—telling his assistant at Kayak, for instance, "I'm a little wired today. I just want to warn you, put on your fireproof suit." But little by little as the summer of 2013 wore on, his ability to catch himself seemed dulled. He'd interrupt an ally of the AGL and he wouldn't seem to notice the man's jaw-hardened glare or to realize afterward that he'd done another blow-by.

On an occasional morning he looked haggard—unshaven, half circles like bruises under his eyes—but for the most part his problems with sleep didn't show. They were serious, however. On top of everything else, he suffered from sleep apnea, and he couldn't tolerate the standard remedy, a CPAP machine, which usually involved wearing a mask to bed. He'd been told his bouts of near mania robbed him of his sleep and that apnea degraded the quality of the little sleep he got. The prior spring, a neuropsychologist had told him that if he didn't fix his sleep problems, he'd probably have a stroke before he turned seventy. The warning had been hovering ever since, seizing him from time to time. He planned to design a better device for apnea, he said, but nothing material had come of this so far. And he also seemed to say he was going to take his hypomania in hand: "I slept two and a half hours last night. I feel great the next morning because I'm on fire. But I know it's not good." And yet he clearly wasn't ready to act. One reason was obvious. "I'm having so much fun these days!" he said, leaving another meeting about Blade.

"So September I turn fifty," Paul remarked one day that summer of 2013, his voice lifting as if to ask himself this question: "It's hard for me to believe, because I think I'm seventeen?" You might have wondered if his plans for Blade's office were merely reproductions of his adolescence, the creation of a venue for his idea of fun, but he had a commercial rationale for Blade-by-night, which he put in a document addressed to Blade.team—that is, to Billo and Schwenk:

> Blade will run monthly meetup parties, invite-only, for selected members of Boston's innovation scene. Our goal is to make these parties one of the best places for engineers and designers and artists to meet. We want Blade to be a destination. Ultimate goal is to have every coder and designer (and VC) between the ages 21-35+ know about Blade, so when they are ready for their next startup, they think to contact us, to see if one of our portfolio companies has an opening, or to see if they themselves are a cofounder candidate.

Paul knew his intended audience. He was now a senior lecturer at MIT's School of Management and was helping to teach a course in which students divided themselves into teams and practiced at creating start-ups. One night a week, Paul coached them in product development and the crafts of branding, team formation, budgeting, fundraising. He taught for no pay except the pleasure of it, and of course the chance to meet coders and entrepreneurs whom he might someday want to hire. He had a special feeling for both the shy and the gregarious youths whose minds teemed, like his, with things to build in software. He sought them out, both at MIT and elsewhere, playing the role of informal and unpaid adviser to half a dozen small teams of young programmers and designers. One of his favorites was a group of four MIT computer science graduates who, though just in their midtwenties, had already created and sold a software company for $70 million. Paul had lunch with them one afternoon to catch up on their latest enterprise. First, though, he had to tell them his own news, his plans for the Blade office.

He was just getting started—"And it turns into a nightclub at night," he was saying—when, in unison, all four young engineers burst out laughing.

"And you just unplug the desk from the wall. Probably in thirty minutes thirty desks will disappear."

"That sounds *awesome!*" cried the young woman of the group.

"And when I put my hand on the puck, the Grey Goose and Kahlúa will light up . . ."

Softly, pensively, as if to himself, one of the young men said, "I want to hang out at this nightclub."

Billo and Schwenk were turning out to be a harder sell. At one meeting, leaning over floor plans with them, Paul pointed to a corner of the office-to-be, saying he wanted a glass-block window there, to face the alleyway beside that old green metal door that he planned to use as

Blade's main entrance. "I want to preserve that edgy look in the alley. I want there to be some mystery, like what's in *there?*"

Billo stared at him. "I'm not really down with the whole scary back door entrance. So I'd rather have a real window there."

Schwenk for his part didn't think an office ought to have a disco ball hanging overhead, at least not during working hours.

In one morning's email to Blade.team, Paul sent Billo and Schwenk a document describing "BLADE.truck." First a photo of a standard black pickup, followed by a photo of the same truck partially "pimped out" (wheels blackened, chrome dimmed). Then the details:

Use for furniture etc and for event equipment. And to have another fun toy to drive, tailgate, demo. We'll lease a nearby garage space 24x7, and let any of us borrow when needed.

Ford Configuration

—F-150 XL 4wd Supercab 6.5' bed EcoBoost 3.5L V6, black running boards, bed liner, black tonneau cover, trailer tow package

—leather seats? cameras? parking sensors?

—steering wheel volume controls? note we're going to rip out dash system and replace with an iPad

Customization

—BLADE graphics in dark grey (large but subtle)

—de-badge (or BLACK), and HIDE any chrome that sneaks into this (SEE ALSO)

—after-market black WHEELS

—rip out the dash system and replace with an iPad, thus, we want minimal stuff ordered

—install Garmin GTU 10 GPS so we can all find it

Questions

—replace dash system with iPad—how can we get outside cameras displayable on the iPad?

—probably rip out the buggy Ford Sync shit [billo: note that the kenwood satnav/stereo/bluetooth/whatever that Safi put in my sprinter is the buggiest slowest piece of shit ever, way worse than any car thing I've seen. So maybe we go totally low end and do everything with iPad integration, but we have to choose carefully.]

—upgrade stereo, amps, sub

—iPhone proclip

—under-car purple lights for effect when parked in our alley at night, maybe color changing to the music :)

—upgrade/add some lighting (but not obnoxious)—note f150 already has an option for interior color changing

—possible extra cameras [billo: integrated camera is likely to be better than any aftermarket]

—USB power ports near tailgate for tailgating

—110 outlets somewhere in the back

—Audio ports to allow snap connect outdoor speakers in back for tailgating

—maybe CUSTOM EXHAUST? for NICER SOUND, but NOT too loud

—possible laser jammers (pme happy to pay for this)

—plate BLADE1

—BLADE Boston (or whatever) logo on side but not too loud

—commercial plates for more parking options? or firefighter or whale watch or fishing?

What else should we consider?

Schwenk wrote back that he didn't think Blade money should be spent on the truck, and certainly not $50,000, the sum Paul had mentioned. Musing over that email, Paul thought it was probably just as well that he hadn't told Schwenk about the likely costs of all the stuff he was planning for Blade's interior—the high-quality speakers and projectors and color-changing lights and all sorts of electronic devices and complex bundles of wiring, which would probably end up costing around half a million dollars.

Soon after Paul sent off his description of the truck, the three Blade founders had a meeting. They talked about various issues, including the desks for the office. Billo said he could get those built inexpensively. Then, just before they parted, Paul said, "Can we talk truck for a minute?"

"I don't think we should do it," said Schwenk.

"Oh, come on, Schwenk!" cried Paul. "Billo just saved us forty grand on desks!" Less vehemently, Paul added, "I'll do it anyway, but I want the name Blade on it."

"It seems crazy to spend fifty grand for a truck that has nothing to do with the business," said Schwenk.

Billo wasn't a worrier, but as the summer wore on, Paul's public recitations about their new company began to trouble him. In an email, he told Paul, "I think it would be better if you backed off a lot on the Blade as music/art pitch. You tend to lead with it when introducing the company, when in reality it will be 5% of what Blade is (or should be)."

Paul sent a mild reply, but he was stung. "I've gotten to the age where I'm not gonna *not* do something I want to do just because someone doesn't like it. Fuck it, I'll do what I want to do," he said one morning soon afterward, striding across the Summer Street bridge toward Blade.

Schwenk *was* a worrier, and Paul's enthusiasm for Blade-by-night had begun to cost him sleep. Schwenk remembered, from a decade ago, reading about a fire in a nightclub in Rhode Island set off by pyrotechnics meant to dramatize a band's performance. One hundred people had died. The band's manager and one of the nightclub's owners went to jail. What if one of Paul's parties got out of hand? By email Schwenk told Paul he didn't like his costly plans for the Blade bar and his talk about hosting parties of 250 people. "I don't want to be involved at my level as a partner if we're not having this be a normal business 95+ percent of the time. I'm also concerned about the risk to me as a partner in this venture if it really turns into your personal night club."

Paul called Billo and Schwenk "my no-men." He said, "They call bullshit on me all the time. I crave their criticism." In truth, he didn't seem to like criticism any more than most bosses, but more than most he had arranged to receive it. And yet for now, as his dreams of Blade-by-day and -night sped on, his no-men represented little more than light touches on the brakes.

One afternoon at the very end of July, half a dozen friends received an email from Paul with the subject header "Graves Light."

> Ok, you know about Shake the Lake, but soon we might have Light the Night as well! (But I don't think the coast guard will allow lasers.)

The next line of Paul's email contained a link to a story in *The Boston Globe* about the impending sale of the lighthouse on the outermost island of Boston Harbor, a towering, weather-beaten old lighthouse fronting the open sea on a pile of rocks called Graves Ledges. Under a photograph of the structure, a caption read "The Graves Island Light Station near the entrance to Boston Harbor has no plumbing or utility services, and getting to the front door requires a climb on a 40-foot ladder." Paul's email continued:

> i am going to place a bid just before auction close in five days don't tell anyone yet!

5

PAUL BID HALF A MILLION DOLLARS FOR THE LIGHTHOUSE AND woke the next morning alarmed. "What the fuck have I done? That's the stupidest thing I've ever done." Remorse was like a little clearing in the sky. Someone offered more for the lighthouse, and Paul felt no temptation to compete. He felt he had been rescued.

Months later, Brenda White laughed over the memory of this misadventure. Sometimes in Paul's presence these days, she would think, "Am I talking to a little boy right now? I sometimes feel like I'd prefer the man." Brenda was still trim, younger-looking than Paul, though she was about his age, near fifty now. "Him buying a lighthouse," she said. "Part of me says, If the guy can afford it, what harm does it do? He'd have ended up giving it away. If I were in a relationship with someone who couldn't afford it, that would be worrisome. But Paul buying a lighthouse? That sort of thing doesn't frighten me, because he can afford it, and something good's going to come out of it."

Brenda had followed Paul, with a few detours, from Interleaf to

Boston Light, to Intuit, and finally to Kayak, which she had joined near its beginning, as employee number fourteen. She was one of Paul's valued QA engineers, by then a mother of two and still very happily married. Some three years later, her husband died suddenly. Brenda was staggered. "I wanted to crawl under a table and unplug myself," she said. Meanwhile, a voice in her mind was saying, "When you're a mother, you have to be strong."

In the aftermath, family and some friends gathered at her sister-in-law's house. Worries had begun to harry Brenda. How was she going to take care of her two kids, how would she keep them housed and clothed and fed? When Paul arrived, he sat down beside her— "in his quiet way," she said. She thought, *This is my employer who* knows *what I'm going through.* Paul didn't have to say anything. Just sitting there beside him, she knew her job was one thing she didn't have to worry about. He'd give her whatever she needed—the freedom to work more often at home, to take time off.

Over the next months she often turned to him for other reassurance, sometimes by text message: "Am I going to be all right?" she'd ask, and he'd reply, "I'm so bullish on you." He always made time to talk. She remembered, "My mother's voice did not assure me. My friends' voices did not assure me. But Paul did. And then it turned romantic. I think they say a year is proper. I think it was actually eight months."

She could begin to list but couldn't rank what drew her to Paul. She felt respect for what he'd accomplished in the world, and for her, he still fell in the category of an attractive man. But what she pictured when she thought of him weren't his looks exactly but his smile and his laugh. She could remember working with him at Interleaf, their computers side by side—and the patient way he'd helped her with her code, and the way he'd worked at his, rewriting, rearranging until it seemed to her that it approached perfection, both in its neatness on the screen and its efficient functioning. His meticulousness had continued, evidently, and extended to his habits at home, Paul making everything line up just so on the shelves in his kitchen and in the silverware rack of his dishwasher. To her these quirks, Paul's "nerdy ways," were charming. It was great sport, pure "nerdy fun," to sit with him at her house or his and trade ideas for things like apps and interface designs, one-upping each other—"That might work, but how about this?"

At Interleaf, Brenda had begun what she later thought of as a search for "inner peace" and had found her way to Buddhist teachings. For her, Buddhism wasn't a religion except in the old sense of the word, religion as a practice, one based on many time-honored techniques, which seemed sensible, even scientific. Her other friends weren't very interested in this, but Paul would always say, "Tell me more. Give me an example."

She remembered, from the time when they first became a couple, trying to help him through what appeared to be a severe panic attack. She couldn't remember the cause or exactly what Paul had said, but he was trembling and he seemed to be speaking to his father, apologetically, fearfully. She rubbed his back, spoke soothing words, and finally helped him take a sleeping pill. He would ask her, "Do you think I'm bipolar?" She knew he hated the label, and she could honestly say she'd never seen him clinically depressed or in a state that struck her as truly manic. His bouts of grandiosity seemed a thing apart, not the product of egotism but of something inborn, chemical. She encouraged him to stick with his medications and also to continue his own meditation practice.

He had told her about the fights of his teenage years and the fury that went with them, all of which was hard to imagine, because it seemed completely out of character. She had seen him truly angry at her just once, and that occasion was notable for his restraint. He wasn't shaking or red in the face. He simply ducked his head, saying in a calm voice, "Hang on." Several times he tried to speak and stopped, and calmly said again, "Hang on."

In every important way, he was the perfect companion for this next part of her life. But for the first five years of their romance, she kept breaking up with him.

For one thing, she was dating the boss, and everyone in the Concord office had to know. *What's Schwenk thinking?* she'd ask herself. Mainly, though, the problem had to do with circumstance and timing. "My kids were in high school, my daughter was twelve, my son fifteen. They had been through the most earth-shattering change of their lives, and I wanted them to have no more change, and bringing Paul into my life—for my life it was good, but not for them." When her father had died, her mother had been "rock-solid there" for her and her siblings. Maybe that was the source of her conviction. Paul wanted more time with her than she could give. Again and again, she felt undone. She would tell Paul, "We shouldn't date. I can't make you happy and my kids happy." Looking back, she said, "I should have been dating someone who didn't have time for me either."

When he and Brenda would break up, Paul used to remove her phone number from the Favorites on his smartphone, and at once he would start going out with other women. He would warn them about Brenda if things seemed to be getting serious, and sooner or later he would end up telling them, "I'm sorry, but Brenda called." He explained, "I was trying to get over Brenda." One could say he had worked hard, even overtime, at this. In February, he had received valentine cards from no fewer than nine other women. So far, though, he hadn't been able to get over Brenda.

In the course of their decades-long and often interrupted conversation, she had taught him the beginnings of a way to quiet himself when he felt irritation or anger rising. He remembered her saying, "Anger is an incredible gift that someone is giving you. It gives you an opportunity to figure out something about yourself." Looked at this way, anger also gave him a choice. When he felt it stirring, he would say to himself, "You can choose *not* to get angry. Would you hit yourself with a hammer?" Adapting general Buddhist practice, he would form an image of feelings that assailed him, usually anger or shame. He would imagine them as tumors, which he was holding in his hand. He would say to himself, "This is that anger, but you know what? It's not around my heart anymore. It's in my hand." He would address the thing, saying, "I'm not ashamed of you, and when I'm ready, I'm going to throw you away."

Boston's narrow roads and notoriously deranged drivers had been a principal laboratory. In the years of phase one, a driver would cut Paul off and he would speed up after the car and return the favor if he could. In phase two, he would stay in his lane and talk to himself, saying, "That's an angry person, and I'm not going to try to get retribution, because they're going to fuck themselves up." Nowadays, in what he thought of as phase three, he'd look at the driver speeding away and think, *I love that person, and if I had their background and chemistry, I would probably cut me off, too.*

Sometimes he wondered if others might not turn the tables on him: "Sometimes I meet people who are so fucking sweet I wonder if they're holding it in. And then if they get angry at me, will I not fucking know?" The thought amused him. What mattered, what felt good, was knowing he'd made progress. Just recently, he had driven a friend to the airport in rush hour traffic, and halfway there she'd told him, "You're amazing. You're the only person I know who doesn't get upset in traffic." The previous winter, his neighbor, an elderly woman who shared a driveway with him, had mistaken reverse for forward and backed her big Mercedes at high speed into the front of his garage. She'd half destroyed the structure. Even worse, the flying debris had damaged his Audi R8, his most expensive, most beloved car, the car he wouldn't drive when it was raining or take to a meeting unless there was valet parking and he knew and trusted the valet. Moreover, this woman and her husband had given him no end of trouble back when he'd been renovating his house. Right after the accident, however, when he came running outside and found the old woman distraught, he told her that she shouldn't worry, insurance would cover everything. The next morning he felt as though he had passed an important test.

Of course, he had to tell Brenda—"I felt really proud," he said. They were a couple again at the time, but only for a while. By May, they had broken up once more. He hadn't deleted her number from his Favorites, though. He'd grown tired of removing it and typing it back in. He might as well just leave it there. About three months later, around the time of his fiftieth birthday, Paul told his current girlfriend that he was sorry, but Brenda had called.

Her circumstances had changed. She had sold her house, which her husband had built and which she had designed in the image of a childhood dream of a house. She had resigned from Kayak. She had loved QA coding, but twenty years of it felt long enough. Her Kayak stock made her financially independent, and now both children were heading off to college. No house, no job and no need for one, no kids except on holidays. She finally had time for Paul, but she was afraid she had pushed him away once too often. She had felt miserable all summer, harboring this thought. When she finally called him, she said, "Can we just hang out?"

The past summer, the eve of his fiftieth birthday, had seemed at times like one of Paul's parties greatly elongated—a bacchanal to celebrate his new beginning with Blade and to mark if not to mourn the end of his fifth decade. It had been interrupted now and then by periods of somber clarity—for instance, in July an email time-stamped 6:24 A.M. and labeled "success": "There is a part of this that feels awful. I keep getting invited to meetings. People want something. And they all project themselves onto me and give me unsolicited advice. I also feel fake. I know that I get too much credit for KAYAK by many people . . . This stupid 'success' right now is an elephant that follows me around. I can't let it block my view or change who I am." But it was as if he would surface and look around for a moment and the next thing you knew, he was trying to buy a lighthouse.

Right around the time when Brenda called, he resolved to take on hypomania again. First he went to see his latest therapist. She had lasted longer than most. She had a medical degree and knew the psychoactive pharmacopeia. Paul came out with a prescription for a fairly new antipsychotic called Saphris, supposed to curb mania in people with bipolar disorder. In the afternoon Paul headed for his psychiatrist's office, in a quiet, antiquated wing of Mass General. Old photographs of psychiatrists hung on the walls of the waiting area. Paul was sitting under their gaze, bent over his smartphone, working on email with both thumbs, when his doctor emerged, a tall man in a dark suit. "Paul," he said.

"Just a minute," Paul replied without looking up. He kept on typing, thumbs flying.

The doctor stood over him. "Paul," he said again.

Paul looked up. "Oh, I didn't see you there."

His psychiatrist thought this little moment significant, Paul distracted and forgetting where he was—a classic symptom of hypomania. "He's very worried about my hypomania," Paul said afterward, striding away toward the parking garage and his next Blade meeting. "He thought my bidding on the lighthouse was bad. He said, 'If we don't fix this, you're going to have a heart attack.' What else did he worry about? I can't remember."

He did remember that his psychiatrist wanted him to try the Saphris, the drug his therapist had prescribed. A few nights later, he took his first dose. The next morning, he felt as if the Lilliputians had pinioned him again. He went out to visit an old friend, who told him he seemed depressed. This reminded him of what that other friend had said years before at Interleaf when Paul was taking lithium, but this time, instead of quitting the drug, he tried to smile, tried to "fake energy." He halved the dose that night, but the next day he felt so weak he couldn't help a friend move some furniture. He couldn't even lift a dining room chair.

He decided to take the drug only on weekends, beginning the next Friday night. On Saturday morning he told Brenda, "I feel insanely groggy." It was a lovely day in Arlington, a day in early September. Brenda said, "Why don't we jump in the pool?" Paul felt somewhat revived afterward but still muted when, in the early evening, he drove south with Brenda along the roads to Hull, roads he'd known since childhood—past the Ford dealership where he and Danny once talked a foolish young salesman into letting them test-drive a brand-new Mustang; past the many police stations and courthouses that Paul had once known all too well; past the sign announcing the town of Hingham—where Paul could smell the salt in the air and the life in the water, where tension seeped away—and finally onto the narrow Hull peninsula. Paul thought the town was like a ship poking its bow out into Boston Harbor.

Hull was the summers he wanted never to end. It was a place where he felt he belonged. "It's seen as the scratchy poor kids who are barely literate," he'd say. It was the kind of seaside spot where you could find a restaurant selling fried Oreo cookies.

He took Brenda to a fancier place, the Red Parrot. It had a second-story outdoor deck. He used to bring his father here when the old man was sinking into forgetfulness. He and Brenda chose a table overlooking Nantasket Beach. She had never been the kind of girl he had ogled with his buddies back in teenage days. She looked demure and wholesome.

As Paul sat there, he felt his energy come surging back, that lovely, scary feeling coursing through his arms. It must be that the drug was wearing off. He'd escaped the hold of that pill he had taken last night. The sensations were as always wonderful, though wonderful in part because they felt dangerous, as if he were standing at the edge of a towering promontory, the master of the world below. For a moment he felt tempted, but he had new reasons to keep this thing in check. He ordered a martini, the only drug handy. He drank it, thinking, *It'll knock me down a little bit.* He was looking at Brenda and taking in the deep shadows over the water, the scents of frying food and salt and beach grass and *Rosa rugosa*. He felt safe with Brenda.

Driving home that night, he decided he'd keep taking his new medication at least for a while.

6

WHEN SCHWENK REALIZED THAT BRENDA AND PAUL WERE A COU-
ple again, he felt relieved of his dire visions—Blade in flames, he
and Paul and Billo in handcuffs. Schwenk told Billo as much: With
Brenda back, Paul's party plans for Blade were bound to quiet down.

"Schwenk knows me pretty well from the outside," Paul once
said. "He can describe my behaviors pretty well. But he doesn't understand why they happen. I don't think Billo does either."

This was true enough. At various times over the years, Schwenk
had heard Paul excuse himself by saying he had to see his therapist,
and he remembered hearing Paul mention that he was "bipolar." But
Schwenk had never inquired about Paul's diagnosis, and Paul had
never talked to him about it. Nor had Billo, though he had guessed
that Paul must suffer from some sort of intermittent psychological
problem. This was one of the things they chose not to know about
one another, and not knowing was easily accomplished, given how
infrequently they met outside of work.

When it came to working together, though, they knew one another well. They didn't have to waste any time discussing their roles in building Blade. Generally, Paul figured, he and Billo would be in charge of strategy, and Schwenk would "make it all real." That is, Schwenk would handle the logistics, all the unforeseen problems and, when necessary and possible, Paul.

They took up residence in a borrowed conference room downtown, not far from the Boston waterfront and the site of the former Chinese restaurant that was slowly turning into Blade. Now and then a seagull perched on the lamppost outside the windows of their temporary office. A table filled most of the room. They posed for a photo there one day: Paul looking up from a blueprint of the Blade office and grinning; Billo bending low over his folded hands and wearing a faint smile, as if interrupted in thought; and the neatly mustached Schwenk, dressed in a T-shirt but looking formal anyway, glancing toward the window as if perhaps calculating the cost of something Paul had just proposed.

They spent many months in their temporary place. Landmark days came early: the landlord's proposed lease agreement, for instance. When it arrived, Paul glanced at the thick document, made a face, then handed it to Schwenk. "Can you read *every* line of this?"

"Sure," said Schwenk with a shrug.

Paul pronounced it another "big moment" when he opened the first Blade bank account. He arrived at their borrowed office carrying the paperwork in what looked like a pizza box. "There should be five hundred grand in that account right now," he said, handing it to Schwenk.

Schwenk took to calling their triumvirate "the three amigos"—with a touch of irony, as if thinking of their differences. Among them, Billo seemed most comfortable with money. He had a lot of it in the bank just now, but he liked the things you could do with it, both spending it and giving it away. Schwenk didn't ever want to be cold and eating squirrels again. He intended to conserve his Kayak millions, and he wanted to make more. As for Paul, half the time he felt he had too much already. He found it exciting to muse on what would happen if he lost it all: "I would want to reenter society as an Uber driver, and that would pay my rent, and I'd start from there. I'd have a very nice car, I'd keep it incredibly clean. It would have iPhone chargers."

Paul said to his partners once, by way of explaining their one clear collective motive for undertaking Blade: "None of us is going to read romance novels on the beach." For himself, he told them, starting companies was like a drug. "I want to keep doing it." Mainly, he thought, he wanted to create teams again, but this time for other people's start-ups. "I don't want to start companies myself, but I totally want to help other people start companies. So in ten years if I'm asked if Blade was a success, I would base it on how many happy CEOs there are of companies we helped start."

Paul put up a million dollars and owned half the company, Billo and Schwenk each put up five hundred thousand for a quarter share. This was their skin in the game. Now it was time to think about selling parts of Blade to outside investors.

Blade would do business on the Internet, where all three of them had worked almost since the advent of e-commerce. Blade companies would be "big bets," Paul said. "No restaurant menus, crap like that." In a good case, several of Blade's start-ups would show early results. Then Blade could easily raise more capital and go on starting companies. Paul usually imagined best cases. At moments his enthusiasm infected even Billo. At a meeting with a lawyer in their borrowed office, Billo spoke of "billion-dollar hits." He said, "I'll be bummed if there's not one in four years."

The lawyer nodded. "You guys are doing big-game hunting."

They'd recruit young monster coders to create the start-ups and young rock stars to manage them. Maybe some would build the Blade founders' ideas, maybe some would come to Blade with ideas of their own. Unlike most incubators, theirs would eschew the "spray and pray" approach and do "seed and feed," guiding start-ups to their first large dose of capital, their "Series A." That is, Blade wouldn't just give a little help and money to a plethora of start-ups, hoping a few would flourish. Rather, they would choose two or three a year, house and nurture the hatchling enterprises for at least six months, and help them get their first substantial financing. In return, Blade would take between 20 and 50 percent of the new companies' shares. And finally, Blade would "kick them out." Paul meant that they'd be asked to find their own offices, but he preferred the harsher phrase. Talk of kicking people out sounded like a promise to investors that the three amigos would be tough and businesslike.

At one point Paul gave his pitch to a very wealthy Bostonian who had expressed an interest in the amigos' new venture, and the man said, "No business plan? No spreadsheet?"

Paul said, "Nope," and afterward remarked, "I was a little arrogant maybe, but it was fun to see a billionaire squirm."

The amigos couldn't know what businesses they were going to hatch until they started hatching them. Their plan for making money was vague of necessity. When describing Blade to potential investors and sometimes even to advisers, Paul countered that vagueness with hyperbole, speaking as if all bets on Blade's success would be guaranteed.

Blade companies wouldn't just be big bets. They would bring the titans of the Internet to their knees: "We'll do an Amazon killer. Probably first a Fidelity one and later a PayPal one."

Recruiting only A-plus people for Blade—that would be no problem. One time, speaking privately, he confessed that he dreamed of lunching with the directors of "the top ten companies in Boston" and telling them, "I will find your best people and take them from you. The reason I'm putting you on notice is not for you to protect them, because I will find them and I will get them. I'm putting you on notice so you can begin to find their replacements."

Most of what they pondered that summer and fall was Blade's financing. First, how much should they try to raise? Paul arranged dozens of meetings in the borrowed conference room and restaurants, soliciting advice from lawyers and investment bankers and principals of other incubators. The counsel they received ranged wildly, from five million to a hundred million. Eventually the amigos settled on twenty million—enough, they figured, to start three companies a year for four or five years.

Where to get the twenty million? They considered several possibilities and settled on venture capital firms, a traditional source of financing for young companies, a source Paul understood, VC money having financed Kayak. Finding VCs who were willing to invest in Blade? That would be no problem either. "When the VCs see we're open, confident, they'll be desperate to get in," Paul said.

The dot-com bust had halved the number of venture firms. There were only about 475 of them operating now, but they still had large effects. Collectively over the past decade, VC firms had deployed about $25 billion and fostered the growth of companies worth something like $3.5 trillion. Practices varied, but in general the business worked this way: The people managing money for pension funds and university endowments and a small number of very wealthy families invest a small percentage of their holdings in a venture fund, with a total worth of anywhere from two hundred million to a billion. The VC firm takes 2 percent of the fund as a yearly management fee and invests the rest in a variety of start-ups and young companies. The VC takes 20 to 30 percent of the profits, if profits materialize.

The business can be lucrative, but it is risky, at bottom a form of gambling, no matter how carefully and cleverly performed. To thrive, a VC has to do a lot better than double the money it invests. If a given fund merely doubles in value over ten years—the usual lifetime of a fund—the yearly return to the limited partners will have amounted to only 7 percent, far too little to satisfy most limited partners, given that an investment in a VC's fund is expensive and illiquid. Limited partners expect about five times their money back over ten years. To get that return, a VC has to make at least a couple of very good bets. As a general rule, about 70 percent of start-ups fail, and 20 percent don't even come close to becoming "5X wins." To make up for the inevitable disappointments, to get that 5X average return, a firm has to look for "home runs"—that is, for individual companies that will turn into wins of at least 20X.

One way around this dismal math is for the VC to invest early on in a company that "exits," by way of a sale or public offering, for a great deal of money, say a billion dollars or more. In the past decade only a small fraction of all VCs had made early investments in even one such company. General Catalyst in Cambridge had joined the club when Kayak was sold. The return on GC's initial investment had been spectacular: In nine years, $5 million had turned into about $450 million. The firm had some other success stories to tell, but Kayak was a brand known to millions. Moreover, GC wasn't only Kayak's first investor but had helped to invent the company. These days when GC went looking for new money from limited partners, the pitch began, "We helped start Kayak."

Paul's old boss and friend Larry Bohn was still a partner at General Catalyst. In February, when Paul had just started dreaming up Blade, Larry had told him across a restaurant table that GC was going to be one of Blade's principal investors. The way Larry put it was: "You have to bring us in."

"Why do I have to?" said Paul.

"You just have to," said Larry.

"We don't owe GC anything," said Paul. "You owe *us*."

"I agree," said Larry. "But you have to bring us in."

There was never much question that Paul would do that, but he wanted at least one other investor. He had three in mind. All belonged to what he called "tier one," and all were more prestigious than GC—"ten times GC," Paul said. This mattered. In the VC business, success bred success. Tier ones tended to get the best "deal flow." That is, a lot of the best entrepreneurs with the best ideas came to tier ones first to ask for help and money. Partnership with one or more tier ones would probably improve Blade's deal flow, too. And Paul had ready access to three of those "A-plus" firms. Two, Accel and Sequoia, had made early and very profitable investments in Kayak, and Paul had long-standing friendships with two of the principals at the third, Greylock. All those firms had headquarters in Silicon Valley, and in the interest of due diligence, Paul led Billo and Schwenk on a scouting trip out there—a trip to Mecca, as Paul put it. They ran their traps at all three firms. Reid Hoffman, the founder of LinkedIn and a principal at Greylock, summarized their aims: "You want to found great consumer companies in Boston and don't want to found them yourselves." He added, "My first advice would be, go and found another one yourselves." But Hoffman called the idea "perfectly coherent." All the West Coast firms seemed interested, Accel especially.

Over the next two months, the amigos settled on the terms they'd ask for. They would sell 30 percent of Blade, to some combination of VCs. The price would be $20 million. If they got that deal, Blade, at its inception, would thus have a total valuation of about $66 million—or $68 million, if you counted the amigos' own investment. By any standard these terms were rich for a company with no tangible assets.

Moreover, the amigos felt they couldn't grant VCs what they were bound to want the most. The great payoffs in venture capital came from making early, prescient Series A investments—investments like General Catalyst's in Kayak, a few million yielding hundreds of millions and sometimes even more. For their $20 million, the VCs would want above all the preferential right to invest in the Blade companies they thought most promising. But to grant such rights would put Blade's whole strategy at risk. When the time came to look for Series A investments, Blade's hatchlings would in effect be captives of the VCs funding Blade. On those grounds alone, the most talented entrepreneurs, the ones the amigos wanted, might well avoid Blade. So the most the amigos felt they could offer VCs was early introductions to Blade companies.

Sometimes when talking to advisers, Paul spoke as if several VCs had already agreed to those terms. Paul Graham, one of the founders of Y Combinator, the country's best-known incubator, was openly astonished at this news: VCs would give Blade all those millions just to *meet* its young entrepreneurs?

———

For Paul, all transactions were negotiations, and the first rule was that you never used the word "negotiation." You always tried to make your counterparty feel there was nothing to negotiate. When you took up two parking spaces in order to protect your car's paint job, you didn't ask the attendant if this was okay. You went up to him and, pointing at another car, you said, "Holy smoke, have you seen those new Corvettes before? Are they rare?" Human beings followed patterns. Get a guy like a parking attendant to step outside his accustomed role by asking him a question—something personal, a question he probably hadn't heard that night—and he was likely to forget his duty to make you repark your car.

You didn't roll down your window and beg the cop to spare you from another speeding ticket. Remembering that cops have high divorce rates, you said, "Officer, I'm sorry, I was on my way to pick up my son. I have a custody issue, and I didn't want to be late." If you guessed right, the cop was apt to pause and look at you and murmur "You're all set" as he turned away.

Or suppose Paul was trying to get himself and Brenda inside a sold-out concert for which he had no tickets. If he let himself look anxious, the guy at the door would stop him, whereas if he walked up portraying authority in his face and step, the door guy would assume that Paul was too powerful to challenge.

Paul called these sorts of tactics "confident technique." Being large in size and bank account didn't hurt, but bullying was anathema, especially if the other party was a woman. Paul once bought a used car for his daughter. He talked the seller down to a price well below the Blue Book value but then he realized, "This woman's really hard up!" And he ended up giving her a thousand dollars more than she'd asked for in the first place. In the end, negotiating with housewives and cops and parking attendants wasn't very satisfying. Paul sometimes visited a car dealership just to practice haggling with salesmen. They were pros in their own right. But they were amateurs compared to the best VCs.

In the event, however, Paul didn't meet a lot of opposition, except from Greylock. One of its senior partners later remarked, "Paul is in the top echelon of people we would finance." But the math didn't work for Greylock. To be the kind of hit they looked for, Blade, with its high valuation, would have to make about $1.6 *billion* in the next ten years. Greylock offered Paul less than half of what he was asking: $4 million for 15 percent of Blade.

In the meantime, Paul had turned to Accel. Without question, it was a tier one, an early investor in a bunch of "unicorns," including

Facebook. In Kayak's early days, Paul had gone to the firm's London office looking for a VC who would help Kayak expand into the European market. He'd met an Accel partner there, a courtly Dutchman named Harry Nelis, and had talked Harry and his partners into investing in Kayak's second round of fundraising, its Series B. Accel had put up $8 million and got back about $200 million. Now Paul flew again to London. He presented Blade to Harry and a group of other Accel partners. He was asked some tough questions, which was fun, a chance to boast about Billo and Schwenk. He also spent five hours touring the vast city on foot. Aching legs gave him a new idea: Smooth Walking, a sensor connected to a smartphone app that would help the user make perambulation gentler on the body. A few days later, Harry agreed in principle to Paul's terms, with some modifications. Accel London would put up $5 million and Accel U.S. another $5 million to buy 15 percent of Blade. Paul emailed the news to Billo and Schwenk.

"Good news!" Schwenk replied.

"Holy shit!" wrote Billo.

But Billo wondered: If Accel was on board, why not try for another tier one? Why not pitch Blade to Sequoia, too? Paul had a pleasant history at Sequoia. Years ago, he and Steve Hafner had gone there looking for a Series B investment, the Sequoia partners had turned them down, Paul had flown to Boston, and then, on the very next day, Paul had flown back, alone and uninvited, and the firm, to its profit, had decided to invest after all. Clearly, Paul wasn't afraid of being turned down if he pitched Blade to Sequoia. He was afraid that if they came on board, there might not be a place for General Catalyst.

Paul often said that a good VC could be very helpful in showing companies the way to profitability, and GC had been more than helpful in getting Kayak built. But being financed by VCs carried liabilities. For one thing, they might pressure you to sell out when you didn't want to, or before you thought it wise. There had been good reasons for GC's wanting to get Kayak sold: to certify that GC was a unicorn creator and to protect its gains against untimely events that might have lowered Kayak's value. As time went on, senior members of the firm got more and more nervous, and Paul gave them some cause for worry. One time, for instance, a bad interaction between alcohol and a new drug he was trying had sent him to the hospital, and by the time the story got back to GC, it had become terrible news: Kayak's CTO had suffered a stroke. In truth, Paul hadn't felt entirely opposed to the sale, but he had felt sad about it. And he blamed GC in part for his sadness. He thought they had pressured him unduly to put Kayak on the market.

Grudges didn't usually stick with Paul. He seemed to be keeping this one alive for the sake of negotiations. Although he sometimes said hard things about GC in private, he didn't like to hear others criticize the firm. One time, Paul and Billo met with a lawyer who repeated an old charge—that GC's managing director, Joel Cutler, had in effect stolen the idea for Kayak. Billo explained why the accusation made no sense from an engineering standpoint, while Paul just stared at the lawyer, inwardly annoyed. Whatever their differences, GC was like family to Paul.

There would have been no Kayak without General Catalyst. Steve Hafner was Joel Cutler's old friend, and it was mainly the two of them who had cooked up the idea. To cut GC out of Blade would be a cruelty. The world of VCs was competitive. Schadenfreude was not unknown. What would people say if Paul English, Kayak's cofounder, chose not to partner with GC again? And what if Blade produced another big hit like Kayak, and GC had no role in it? In the end, Paul simply had to face the fact: "I can't fuck over Joel."

This didn't mean he couldn't use the weapons he'd assembled.

Joel was a worthy adversary, "a powerful snake charmer," Paul once told Billo and Schwenk. When Paul sent Joel his conditions for investing in Blade, he wrote, "We have a top-tier investor ready to sign the attached term sheet, where they will put in $10m of the total $20m that we will raise." He didn't name Accel. He didn't think that GC and Accel would collude in trying to lower the price for a piece of Blade, but why not just eliminate that possibility?

Joel emailed to ask if he might offer a few suggestions about modifying the deal.

Paul replied: "Yes let me know your thoughts. I would prefer we do this quickly, as I have a couple other high quality investors breathing down my neck and I want to tell them to go away."

7

MAYBE BECAUSE THE OFFICES OF VENTURE CAPITALISTS ARE ALL theaters of risk, they tend to be well appointed and to feel sedate. GC had a front reception desk staffed by well-dressed women, lots of gleaming hardwood, a visible hierarchy that put young associates and female secretaries in cubicles on the interior and partners—all male—on the perimeters, in offices with doors and windows. In the main conference room, one rested one's elbows on the polished wood of a Thanksgiving-size table, a lot like the tables in all the VC conference rooms Paul had visited in the past few months. And there were cushioned chairs that swiveled and a giant video monitor for teleconferencing and for showing PowerPoint decks, and a wall of windows opening on the bare branches of Cambridge in December.

Middle-aged GC partners and young subordinates filled the seats—all male and most of them dressed sans neckties and jackets, in the mode of trying-to-look-casual-in-business-clothes casual. Billo was the fellow who looked as though he wished he weren't there.

Schwenk had a routine doctor's appointment and hadn't come, to Paul's consternation. But really the show belonged to Paul and Joel Cutler.

That it was to be a show was clear enough already. A few days before, the amigos had stiffened their terms. No members of the VC firms would be allowed to sit on Blade's board. Earlier that morning, Paul and Billo had been sitting in a small private room at General Catalyst and Joel had stuck his head in the door and asked Paul, "Could you do me a favor? To make this less inflammatory? If you could *not* mention that there won't be any VCs on the board?" And Paul had said, "Sure."

There was nothing for Paul to worry about today. And yet once inside the conference room, he felt, as he still sometimes did in spite of Saphris, that he had "the fire thing going." If you knew him in that mode, you could tell that he was trying to look perfectly at ease, sitting sideways in his chair, an arm slung over the back of it. He looked sidelong at the wires running across the tabletop to speakerphones, and announced to no one in particular, using the present tense instead of the future, "At Blade we drill holes in our tables and the wires go underneath." He was hoping for a fight, or at least a little pushback.

Joel sat at the head of the table, a small, bald man wearing a little wry smile. Joel was a quipster, a witty man and a fast talker. But no one spoke as fast as Paul today. "It's all yours," Joel said to Paul.

The sum total of Paul's presentation, indeed of Blade's business plan, was contained in ten slides. Slide one: a montage of photos of the three amigos and a few sentences about his two lieutenants. "So if there's something fucked up in the organization, he fixes it," Paul said of Schwenk. "He's the anti-me. He's the one who fixed what I did wrong at Kayak." He turned to Billo: "Billo is the best I've ever known at building a team of youngsters and people with graying hair. I think when people visit Kayak, they think it's pretty special. Billo's mobile team was even more special."

Slide two was "the Blade Bench," a listing of people and firms they would hire for jobs such as marketing. "I will hire a full-time recruiter," said Paul. "That person will sit next to me. I'm known a bit as a recruiter." Slide three was "Why Boston?" The answer, mainly, was MIT. "There are twenty-five thousand existing start-ups that were started by MIT people," Paul said. "Three million people in the United States today are employed by start-ups started by people at MIT. They produce two *trillion* in revenue. MIT dominates, it's much bigger than Stanford, than Harvard. The fact that I'm on the faculty at MIT will be very useful to us."

By the time he hit slide four, "Blade Approach," Paul was talking so fast he was slurring his words. "We will be co-founders in ten companies, e-commerce, all big-bet companies, no restaurant menus, we'll do companies that take on Fidelity."

"Slow down here," said Joel. "Take a breath." And Paul obeyed, but soon went on just as rapidly, until he came to the subject of what would happen when a Blade company got off to a promising start and the VCs crowded around, vying to make the Series A investment. "Pause," said Joel to Paul, and then, turning to the table, Joel told his troops: "Ask Paul now, because this is the main issue. How do we get enough of the hatched companies' Series A to make it worth our while?"

A short silence followed, which Paul filled: "There are things I'll promise you and Larry over a beer that I can't put in a contract." He had turned his chair and was facing Joel. "I can't put in a contract that you have the first right of refusal. It would hurt my ability to bring in the best CEOs."

"Talk to *them*," said Joel, gesturing toward the rest of the table.

Paul obeyed, turning again in his chair and looking around. "In general, I expect and hope that GC will have an intimate relationship with all the Blade companies."

Then Paul carried on with his pitch, dropping names now and then. Everyone in the room would know that "Michael" was Michael Moritz, a famous partner at Sequoia, also that "my friend Reid" was Reid Hoffman of that other tier one, Greylock. Paul told the table he had been an entrepreneur in residence at Greylock. This was purposeful name-dropping. In his mind he was telling the audience: *Guys, if you want to ride on this train, you better pay in cash.*

Joel got the message. He smiled. "Greylock's great," he said. "But if Larry hadn't brought you over here that day, you'd still be doing some middleware company." This was a private joke. It summoned up a bit of Kayak history, reminding Paul that he had been working on a dull project at Greylock before the fateful day when Larry Bohn had asked him to come to GC and Paul had met Steve Hafner. In other words, Joel was saying: "You owe us, Paul." Several of the senior people at the table chuckled.

Paul smiled.

Joel said, "Give us an idea of the kinds of firms you're talking to. Our cousins in this."

"Sure." Paul said he'd met with a "superangel" (a wealthy individual investor) and eight VC firms. He didn't offer any names. He wasn't going to tell them yet that Accel was all but signed up, and he was never going to say that Greylock had balked at his terms. Paul wasn't actually lying. He really had talked to principals at eight firms and to a lieutenant of a superangel. His last claim bent the truth a little, though. One investor had mused about what kind of terms his company could get if they put up the whole $20 million. A hypothetical proposition at best, which Paul converted to: "There was one firm that offered to do *all* of the funding."

Larry Bohn cried out. "And at a higher valuation? Gimme a hand-kerchief! I'm going to have a nosebleed!"

Paul was still smiling, happily now. "Joel says it's a ridiculous valuation. I've said all along that we don't want stupid money." Stupid money came from passive investors with no expertise in creating companies. "But looked at another way, stupid money's not so bad."

Then one of the young associates piped up. Paul had explained that he would find rock star founders for Blade companies and Blade would own 50 percent of the equity in each of them. The young man said, "We work really hard to find great founders. Can you find ones who are willing to give up fifty percent? Because *we* don't."

Joel stepped in quickly: "Don't forget. He's hatching them." In this case, "hatching" meant that Blade would be investing a lot of intellectual capital as well as money, and even providing teams to help founders start their companies.

But the young man's question was something very like pushback, at last an occasion Paul could rise to. Paul's smile brightened. Great founders, he said, could be persuaded to part with most of their equity in order to build a great company. He touched his breastbone: "I'm very happy that I ended up owning only six percent of Kayak."

One usually thinks of money as the source of things other than humor, but this remark set the table on a roar. Everyone was laughing, and Paul was grinning, his face reddening.

The talk grew increasingly desultory. Finally, Joel said, "If any of you disagree with what Paul's saying, tell Paul. Because he loves a fight." But no one broke the silence that followed, and Joel adjourned the meeting.

Outside, Joel said, "This is so unconventional. I doubt there are three people in the world we'd do this with. But Silicon Valley would leap at it. To have Paul English covering the Boston market for them?"

One wonders how Paul's proposition would have been received elsewhere, perhaps by a man on the street outside. *What does Blade do? asks the man. Paul says, We're going to create e-commerce companies that make things, but we're not sure exactly what they'll make. Well, asks the man, who are the people who are going to make those things? We're not sure about that either, Paul replies. But they'll be really good at making them, whoever they are. And then Paul asks the man if he'd like to invest $20 million to buy 30 percent of this enterprise.*

It seemed as though the two VC firms were agreeing to something like that. They would give Paul and Billo and Schwenk $20 million, and for collateral they would receive little more than air and résumé. And yet somehow Paul had made them, or at least General Catalyst, feel that he was doing them a favor. There weren't a lot of other places in the world where a transaction like this could happen. It could make sense only within a system in which money was so abundant and unequally distributed that the people who owned most of it could afford to chase the possibility of their money becoming not just a little more money, but a great deal more.

You occupy an odd position as a VC. You must pick your bets carefully to succeed. At the same time, you diversify your bets so that no single bad one ruins you. Twenty million was a fortune in the common world, the world of salaried human beings, but it was just a small fraction of the average venture fund. If Blade failed, Paul and Billo and Schwenk would lose some money but they'd hardly be bankrupted, nor would GC.

In this system, the cascade of risk was limited, the hopes unbounded. It was a system of insubstantialities. When the basic deal was struck, GC and Accel didn't know anything about Blade's investments because, for the moment, neither did Paul or Billo or Schwenk.

All the hopes of astonishing rewards rested on Paul and his lieutenants. There was nothing else for them to rest on, and this was probably just as well, for Blade at least. At this stage of their enterprise, Paul would likely have had a harder time raising $20 million for a specific plan than for an intangibility. For now, VCs were bound to find him most attractive when he talked about big bets without getting into details. And Paul knew it—hence his talk about creating companies that were bound to *kill* all sorts of corporations in the Fortune 500.

Months ago, conferring with Billo and Schwenk, Paul had said they'd raise money on their "pixie dust." Betting on Paul was partly a matter of betting on his past, of course. But he also had qualities in the present that were unusual, and for Internet companies, instrumental. He was a bridge between the business world and the mysterious world of software engineering, where things were made that had become essential to almost everything that people used, to stoves and cars as well as rocket ships. Paul was a figure in Boston's start-up scene. ("A legend," one young acolyte had said, causing Schwenk to cry out in soprano glee, "A *legend?*") Young entrepreneurs called Paul all the time asking for advice, and he was generous with it. And he wasn't only teaching at MIT. The head of electrical engineering there was asking him for advice on how to make the department more "entrepreneurial"—and also evidently angling for a donation. When Paul gave a pizza party at MIT one evening that winter, more than 350 students showed up to chat with him. Paul didn't exactly *own* MIT, as he liked to say when pitching Blade, but he had great access to the kinds of smart young engineers that every corporation coveted. A senior partner at Greylock called Paul "a great recruiter, a Pied Piper for young engineers," and added—this seemed significant—"He's very young at heart." The Greylock partner said, "We would have loved to invest in this new thing of Paul's."

Joel Cutler allowed himself at times to reminisce about Kayak.

For his firm, it had an importance beyond the money and prestige it conferred. "You need these romantic successes," he said. He added, "That's why we need to do this." Joel also said, of successes like Kayak's, "There are very few guys who do it again." He added, "There are very few guys who are *fifty* who do it again. But we're going to put our money down on Paul and Billo and Schwenk."

Mainly, he was putting it down on Paul. Joel said: "Paul's brilliant. There's the dark side, and the bright side. Paul, when he's focused and on, it's magic. He's so brilliant, has so much energy, such clear thinking. Then there's the opposite side of genius. He comes and goes. At every major milestone with Kayak, he would work maniacally and then disappear. Paul is a remarkably special person, a genius, forward thinking, exhausting, exhausted, focused, unfocused, so complex. He's smart enough to know he needs Billo and Schwenk. I always thought of Paul as an artist, this tortured guy who needed to get himself in a frenzy to be able to paint a picture. He's just a picture of complexity."

Back in GC's conference room, Paul had ended his slide show with a black-and-white photo of the Channel Building. Blade's windows, still plain and grimy in fact, were colored purple in the photo, thanks to Photoshop. It was a picture made of fact and fantasy, a little like the idea for Blade, a little like a video game, a little like market capitalism, a little like money for those who have more than enough.

8

BILLO AND SCHWENK ARE SITTING ONE DAY IN THE SMALL CONFER-
ence room that General Catalyst has set aside as a temporary office for Blade. The two men bend over their laptops, Billo working
on plans for what might become the first Blade company, Schwenk
examining the latest bills for furniture that will be installed in the
Blade office. "Oh, boy. Paul's custom couch. Want to know how
much?" says Schwenk.

Billo keeps staring at his computer screen. "I don't want to know."

"Twelve thousand dollars," says Schwenk.

"Tell them *no*," says Billo.

"Paul already said yes."

Schwenk pauses, peering at his screen. "Oh, that doesn't include
the cushions," he says cheerily.

"Or the upholstery," mutters Billo.

"This includes the backlights. Whatever they are. Know anything
about that?" says Schwenk.

"I'm not paying attention," says Billo, eyes still on his machine.

Paying attention was Schwenk's job, after all. He was often at the site itself, the as yet unheated four thousand square feet of half basement that was gradually becoming Blade. Winter had settled in. The cold seemed to travel upward, through the concrete slab that hung just above high tide and into the soles of your shoes— you'd wiggle your toes to make sure they were still there. At the weekly construction meetings, big-handed men dressed in parkas and hooded sweatshirts sat at a rickety table with Schwenk and Paul and various subcontractors and the architect, revising and re-revising the plans and the schedule. Schwenk had installed a security camera outside the green door, now that there were tools and materials inside. Schwenk was keeping track of all the building costs, already well beyond budget.

The meeting over, Schwenk headed out for coffee, to warm up. On Summer Street, pedestrians hunched their shoulders against the north wind blowing in off Boston Harbor. It felt as if it came from northern Maine, or Greenland. Schwenk thawed out at a Dunkin' Donuts a block or so up the street, musing for a time on his garden, now buried under snow out in central Massachusetts.

Paul once described the three amigos' roles in Blade to a potential investor, and Billo broke in, saying, "And Schwenk supplies the cold water." Schwenk set limits on this function, though. In his philosophy, you could complain all you wanted about the astonishing inefficiency of union rules at a construction site, but if they defined the way things were done, you adapted to them. The same went for managing your boss. You should offer your opinions, but not constantly. "Constructive information, versus constant complaint," Schwenk said. "I couldn't work for someone who couldn't bear criticism. I tell him what I think. Paul's the boss, so he'll decide." He had long ago told Paul what he thought about the nightclub features of the office. Blade-by-night was at best a small part of their business, and a large part of the office cost.

But was it possible that the whole enterprise, nightclub included, might just work?

Schwenk looked surprised at the question. He might have been asked if his name was Schwenk. "Oh, it'll work," he said. "He'll *make* it work." He shrugged. "Paul is something. Paul is Paul. You've just gotta roll with it. He can be a pain in the ass, but I'm sure I irritate him, too."

2014. A new year, and many little things were making Paul happy, like the design of the single-serving coffeemaker he and Brenda bought: "I thought it was just a gimmick, but now I see why it's taking over the world." In spite of the antimania drug, he was still the sort of engineer who might apply a Band-Aid designed for fingertips and, staring at it, say, "I love a good invention. Cutting my finger was like a minus two, but discovering this Band-Aid was like a plus five."

In the meantime, Paul seemed all but untouched by events that would have made most people hide in embarrassment. No other donors had joined him to support the American Gun League. The campaign had never really gotten started, and now it was time to begin folding it up. Considering all the favors he'd called in, the quarter of a million dollars he had spent, the time he'd consumed, this should have been a blow. But for Paul, it seemed like just a morning's bother. Too bad the idea hadn't worked, but it was still "a big idea," important for the country. He'd get back to it someday.

He and his little Road Wars team assembled at his dining room table one last time, devised some modifications, and placed the game in the App Store. Paul arranged publicity, but the app did not catch on. Only a few hundred people downloaded it. And so, after two years and somewhere between $100,000 and $200,000 spent, Paul put the software into "maintenance mode." A pessimist might have said he would have done better buying a lighthouse. He chose to look on the positive side. The game had worked for him—no speeding tickets for a year. And helping to design and program the app with friends had been like playing in the Latin School jazz band. That alone was worth the price.

Things were failing all around Paul lately, or so it would have seemed to an objective eye. And yet he had this curious ability, that he could lose so many battles and not feel that he was losing. It helped of course that he always had a lot of projects in progress or in mind. If you looked at matters through Paul's eyes, you'd see that his recent failures were actually small blessings. He'd been feeling a little "overextended." It had been time to "rebalance" anyway. For a year and a half, the AGL had represented his only big civic/philanthropic project. He didn't have another in prospect or in mind. There wasn't room. Blade was all-consuming now.

The construction schedule for the office had slipped and slipped and slipped again. As a rule, Paul found his equanimity in speed. In this case, he had resorted to the illusion of speed, which he created by naming a succession of unrealistic dates. In March, he had said the office would be ready by July or August. By August, it was December. In October, it was looking like March. And so the longed-for date had never seemed all that far away. Now, in winter, he was still elaborating the design of the hybrid office/nightclub.

It's said that computer programmers tend to share with musicians a keen spatial and temporal sense, a sense for patterns. Certainly, many programmers have both a taste and a talent for music. Paul had been a good amateur musician and a better arranger of music, and he still loved music for itself, all of it, from Bach to techno. The office he imagined was filling up both with sound—the DJ booth, the stage, the speakers spread across the open ceiling—and also with original artworks by local artists, which he would buy and rent. And there would be events on weekends—lectures about technology for the benefit of artists, sculpting demonstrations for software engineers. And there would be joint creations, such as the "Collaboration Fountain," which would float in front of Blade's windows in the Fort Point Channel. He had begun drawing up a spec. It read in part: "The fountain runs on a tethered floating dock, maybe 8x8 feet, with a grid of 3x3 (or 2x2) vertical water jets, each of those 9 (or 4) jets which can be set at various heights and colors via a custom mobile application, so that people can control the fountain from their own phones."

You could have read this and imagined collaboration turning to disunion: an art student and young coder who have found a few too many of their favorite beverages through the magic of the Blade bar's hockey puck, looking through the windows at the floating fountain and dueling for control of those vertical water jets.

Paul had serious intentions, though. He was trying to make a commercial office that would be a work of art, a place where many of the things he loved could be assembled, a fusion of his multiple enthusiasms, for teams and music, fine art and first-rate software, parties and hard work, old friends and new. He couldn't stop himself. One of his friends, a distinguished photographer, recalled accompanying Paul to dozens of the venues at Art Basel in Miami and remembered being astonished when Paul—an engineer, an entrepreneur with a gift for making money—began assembling artworks of his own in the air, assemblages of video and painting and music and computer programs.

At long last, on the evening of May 16, 2014, you could stand on the Summer Street bridge and watch the pastel-colored lights changing hues in Blade's tall windows. Not all the parts of Paul's fantasia were working perfectly inside, and some he'd never bother with, but the dungeon was transformed—suffused with natural light by day and enchanted-looking after dark, a sky full of city lights in the windows, throbbing lights and shifting shadows on the dance floor. Blade-by-night had opened with a spring party. Half of Kayak engineering came. So did the retiring governor of Massachusetts, who said, when asked why he was there, that he would soon be looking for a job. Even better entertainments were to come. The masked costume party, for instance, where hired circus performers circulated in the crowd, among them a contortionist who spent the evening wrapping herself around the shoulders of startled guests.

Blade-by-day was also open for business.

9

ON AN EVENING IN 2010, DONALD KNUTH—TALL, UNSTOOPED, white-haired—rose to a lectern in a San Francisco hall and delivered a paper to the TEX Users Group. The occasion was a birthday party for Knuth's grand typesetting system. TEX was thirty-two years old, remarkable longevity in the world of software. But, Knuth said, he had "an earth-shaking announcement": TEX's day was done, he declared. For some time, he had been working in secret on its successor. In moments, the audience was laughing. It was plain that Knuth was offering not a technical talk but a parody of the kinds of overwrought announcements that these days seemed to accompany the marketing of every new piece of software or digital device. Knuth's imaginary new version of TEX was, to borrow from the lingo of the era, "a smorgasbord of awesome," an all-purpose tool, which would revolutionize every aspect of everybody's life. It wouldn't just create beautiful documents to look at, but documents you could hear and even *feel*. Among many, many other things, it would both create and arrange the shipping of industrial products to consumers, while accommodating *an interactive cookbook*, which would interface with your stove and pantry and fridge and prepare your meals automatically, using the ingredients on hand or, if need be, ordering others online.

Knuth amused the crowd and seemed to be amusing himself, but the talk had a wistful undertone. At one point, he said, "In the Internet Age, nothing over thirty months old is trustworthy or interesting." It was a line too accurate for humor. Here was a living symbol of the marvel and complexity, indeed the beauty, of computer science, laughing with irritation at a part of the world he had helped to create.

The most visible part of that world by 2014 was its commercial products, and especially the mobile app. In 2008 about one hundred million people had owned smartphones. By 2014 about two billion were carrying them everywhere, including to bed, and apps to exploit those multipurpose devices now numbered in the millions. Mobile apps now represented the foundations of billion-dollar and multi-billion-dollar companies, including some that had grown as fast as any in history. "A vibrant era," one VC called these past six years.

Around the time when Blade began, the market capitalization of the ten largest U.S. Internet companies was about $1 trillion. The fifteen most popular social networking sites accounted for about half of that, even without adding in some of the capital invested in Google and Yahoo, which controlled a number of purveyors of electronic societies. Facebook alone was valued at more than $200 billion. And many billions more were flowing in, a lot of it to buy advertising for video games and social media sites that might someday make money by selling advertisements themselves. Universities and big companies and even municipal authorities were offering courses in entrepreneurship, running "start-up accelerators," staging competitions known as hackathons.

There seemed no end to the church of entrepreneurship. Becoming an entrepreneur was about more than money, about more than starting companies. It was about finding the courage to discover the genius locked inside you. It meant finding your brand, a term that no longer applied just to breakfast cereals or corporations, but also to the self. If you were unbranded, did you even exist?

And yet the vast majority faced long odds, rather like the odds against would-be movie stars or kids in city playgrounds who dream of becoming pros. To become a real entrepreneur, to turn your app into a profitable company, you needed a great deal of luck, and sooner or later you needed investors, and for most would-be founders, significant sums were hard to find. Joel Cutler and his colleagues at General Catalyst were obliged to turn down about 250 plausible enterprises for every one they financed, and even among the selected, seven of ten would probably fail and only one become a large success—and that only with luck. Selection could seem like a painful process even to a hard-hearted VC. Joel Cutler described it this way: "Someone comes to you, opens himself up to you, utterly passionate about this thing he wants to do, asks, 'Would you give me money to do it?' And if you say no, it's as if you're saying no to the person."

The amigos posted a public invitation on the Blade website. It read in part: "Blade is interested in software and hardware that will be used by tens of millions of users. Interested? Reach out to us to hear more." The invitation also said that Blade would finance "a few technology start-ups a year." The warning was implicit, but there was a world of longing out there on the Web.

The proposals rolled in. Several dozen opened like loud and cheerful voices at the door. "Hello Blade!" "Hi There!" "Good evening!" "Hi guys—cool space, I'd love to learn more." Some would-be founders introduced themselves at once: "Hi! My name is . . ." One began: "I am a creator. I am an entrepreneur. I am a woman."

Most were men, and most were young. There were students still in college or in business school, also recent graduates and people somewhere in the span of middle age who wrote that they were restless working at the desks of other people's companies. Some had started companies before. One called himself "a serial founder" and claimed a decent record: "2 successes, 1 failure—all made me stronger." One said he'd won and lost a fortune, and was starting out again. None seemed to lack passion: "Daily, I create notes on my smartphone of future business opportunities and it gets my blood pumping." "Seeing the description of reaching 'tens of millions of users' fits the concept I've been working on."

The Blade application asked candidates to describe the problems they intended to solve and not the solutions they'd devised, but many couldn't resist. Several had created electronic versions of the glossy brochure, "pitch decks," for this purpose. Ideas were *awesome, revolutionary, disruptive, game-changing*, and, in one email, "extraordinary, futuristic in vision, massive," also "exciting, disruptive at its core, and universally game changing." Some wrote that they were only in "the concept stage" or "the ideation stage." Others had already created an early version, a beta, of their product. Nearly all were "excited" to tell Blade about their plans.

All would continue the process of converting the culture from analog to digital. They'd be moving in, that is, on "spaces ripe for disruption." The fragmented state of healthcare in America. "The antiquated, agent-based system for buying and selling real estate." The lack of "video chat" for consumers trying to contact businesses. The need to connect "busy professionals with great barbers to provide on-demand, in-home, in-office haircuts saving customers time and hassle."

There were plans for an online tool to help people replace lost and stolen stuff. For a "mobile recording studio" that professional musicians could access on their smartphones in order to create new ringtones for the billions of users of smartphones. For a better kind of automated pet door in homes with small animals. For replacing "posters, art prints, and other wall decor with an intelligent high-resolution display." The frustrations of parking in a city could at last be solved: By an app for renting private spaces when they weren't in use. By an app for letting drivers locate vacant public spaces in real time. By a mobile valet service; call or email ahead and people will come and park your car for you, assuming they don't steal it. There was a "comparison engine for fashion" and a plan for connecting "sophisticated and savvy shoppers" with the next "it" handbag. Also a means to let young women professionals join "the sharing economy" and rent out the designer clothes they wore just once or twice.

Most inventions are built on others. Remarkable inventions are rare. The smartphone qualified as one of those, a marvel of combinatory technology, the technology on which most of the proposals depended. The swarms of new ideas for social media apps were all so clearly inspired by Facebook as to make acknowledging the fact redundant. Dating, for example. Does that boy or girl you see across the room find you attractive, too? Are you too shy to find out in old-fashioned ways? There was already an app in development to help with this. All it needed was seed money.

With the right online facility, one petitioner wrote, it would now be possible to make an online game in ten minutes or less. The time was also right for "an online cannabis order and delivery service." Convenience stores could not be allowed to stand; they failed to be aligned "with the way we (urban dwellers) now live our healthy and examined lives." And there was an urgent need for an app to aggregate the news: "No one our age has the time or patience to read a newspaper."

Twentysomething entrepreneurs seemed to think of themselves as a little nation. Perhaps they were, and maybe they were busier than anyone in human history, thanks to all the experiences that one could have online. An app was needed, one applicant wrote, to deal with the problem of too many apps, too many experiences. But what if, once sorted out, those experiences still left a person unsatisfied? One Blade suitor wrote: "The problem I am trying to combat is the inability for people in today's society, to make actual human contact. Whether it is because we are too busy, we are somewhere unfamiliar or we simply lack the social skills, many relationships are maintained through computer screens and online connected devices. We don't think about it but there is something to be said for having a face to face conversation and doing activities with another person." A prototype of an electronic solution existed, but the amigos would have to wait to hear about it. Unlike a number of other Blade suitors, this one obeyed the instructions on the website. "My solution is . . . I was paying attention, I won't tell you about this yet."

Paul read nearly all the applications to Blade, both the public and private pleas, and wrote a stream of gentle rejection slips.

Within months of the opening party, he and Billo and Schwenk had found, through private channels, three fledgling companies. There was Wigo, an app that would make it easy for groups of college students to let one another know where they were partying tonight. Bevy was to be a luxury item; it would combine hardware and software in a sleek little box that would let you organize, store, and share the infinity of photographs and videos that came your way. Classy was to be an online marketplace for used textbooks, but Paul and Billo and Schwenk decided rather quickly that it would never fly. So they sent its CEO away and brought in Vinayak Ranade, their old favorite from Kayak, who wanted to start an enterprise called Drafted.

It would create an informal marketplace of companies in need of software personnel and of people willing to recommend colleagues who might fill those needs.

Maybe all the fledglings, or two or one, would become a real company, but none could reasonably have been described in the terms Paul had used a year ago to describe Blade start-ups. None looked, that is, like a PayPal or Amazon or Fidelity killer.

PART V

THE AMERICAN

1

ON A LATE SUMMER NIGHT IN 2014, PAUL BOARDED A VAN OUTSIDE the Pine Street Inn, Boston's largest homeless shelter. There was a lot of stuff inside the van—jerry cans of hot soup, boxes full of sandwiches, hampers of clean underwear and socks. So the seating was a little cramped in the rear, where Paul sat asking questions of his guide, a doctor named Jim O'Connell.

The light and shadow of the city washed across the windows and the faces in the van. Paul leaned toward Dr. O'Connell, murmuring "Inter-esting, inter-esting" as the doctor spoke. For years Paul had been copying his hero Tom White and giving money to programs for the homeless. Lately, he'd been thinking that he should give more. Tonight he was doing research. He'd been told by people he trusted that if he wanted to know about this problem, he had to meet O'Connell. The doctor was sixty-five. He had spent the past thirty years ministering to homeless patients while helping to create an organization—Boston Health Care for the Homeless—and a host of facilities just for them, including emergency shelters, a walk-in clinic, a residency program at Mass General, and a respite hospital with 108 beds.

The doctor told Paul that eight thousand people were homeless in Boston on any given night. Most were housed by the city in motels or shelters, but about three hundred lived on the streets: "In England, they call it sleeping rough." Vans from the Pine Street shelter had been visiting Boston's rough sleepers for thirty years.

The van wound through downtown. Some stops were brief, Paul watching out the windows as the doctor and the driver's assistant climbed out to check on people sleeping in the city's crevices. They lay under small heaps of blankets on sidewalks, in the doorways of shuttered businesses, on loading docks. Paul watched as the doctor approached them with his flashlight and called to the sleepers by name, saying, "It's Jim O'Connell," and groggy faces, usually smiling, hair in tangles, emerged from under the blankets.

The van made longer stops at sites where crews of homeless people had camped for months and even years. When the van pulled up at these after-dark encampments, Paul got out and watched as little groups, mostly men, came out of the shadows, the van's driver and his assistant offering them the soup and sandwiches, the underwear and clean socks, while a woman named Robyn, a friend of the doctor's along for the ride, was dispensing Dunkin' Donuts gift cards. These, she explained to Paul, conferred the right for the homeless to use the restaurants' bathrooms—"the right to shit," she said. Paul listened in as the doctor chatted with his patients, checking their medications, urging them to come to the walk-in clinic at Mass General tomorrow. It seemed to Paul the doctor knew all of them, and they knew him: "He's a homeless whisperer," murmured Paul.

At one stop Paul found himself facing a row of benches beside

Fort Point Channel, right across the water from Blade, the purple lights in its windows stretching across the darker water. Reflexively, Paul wondered, *Did they do this on purpose?* Would a plea for a donation follow? None did. When Paul pointed across the water at Blade and said, "That's where I work," the doctor was clearly surprised. This was a favored nighttime refuge for the homeless. It had benches, sea air, and one of the city's few public bathrooms not far away, inside South Station.

Stop followed stop, each with its streetlamp-lighted images of misery. There was a psychotic woman with frightened eyes wearing a knapsack—"She's terrified of men," the doctor said to Paul. "If I get near her, she'll start screaming."

In front of a defunct bar called Hurricane O'Reilly's, there was a man with a wispy white beard in a wheelchair who was living out old age on the sidewalks, fending off various lethal ailments with a small pharmacy of medications that he kept in a plastic bag. A garrulous, gregarious fellow who said he used to be lead singer in a band and, to prove it, sang a song for the doctor and his company. Paul listened with his arms folded on his chest, in him a pose of unease; when the man finished, Paul lifted his hands and applauded softly.

There was a boy who came suddenly, silently, out of the dark reaches of a street and into the pool of light surrounding the van. The boy wore jeans, sneakers, a black jacket, a black baseball cap, a black knapsack—all as if, it seemed to Paul, he meant to make himself invisible. And why wouldn't he, given what Dr. O'Connell had said about how people prey on the homeless and how the homeless prey on each other? In what seemed to Paul like one fluid movement, the boy swooped in toward the rear of the van, grabbed a sandwich, and glided away, and by the time Paul thought of trying to talk to him, the boy had disappeared back into the shadows.

Homelessness rounds for Paul tonight were like viewing his hometown upside down. People wrapped in blankets sleeping on benches over at Fort Point, right across the water from the place where he hoped to start successful, if not billion-dollar, companies. People who lacked the right to shit making camp two blocks away from the lighted skyscrapers of the Financial District and the huge rectangular plinth that houses the New England branch of the Federal Reserve. To survive without a home required technique, like woodcraft, it seemed—knowing how to let oneself into temporarily vacant places like ATM lobbies, knowing where to find a bathroom and a modicum of safety, knowing where to hide one's gear, knowing when one had better leave a sanctuary in the morning. From his early teenage years, Paul had the freedom of Boston's streets. He remembered the time when a gang of kids tried to run him over, and the time, late one night near City Hall, when he was mugged, a knife at his throat. Where would that boy who swooped in for a sandwich hide when, in a few months, these streets were transformed into alleys between snowdrifts?

A hopeless feeling began to settle on Paul. It was frustrating for an engineer to look at things that were hard to fix. What were the causes of homelessness? he asked the doctor, in between stops, in the back of the van. Bad luck for some, the doctor said, and for most others, alcoholism, drug abuse, mental illness, dreadful childhoods. Couldn't something be done at least about the substance abuse? Paul asked. The doctor replied, "Those who got sober, I can almost name all of them over thirty years, and almost all of them had lives before. Most of the people we've met tonight never worked."

What would O'Connell do if he had the resources to launch a grand antihomelessness campaign? The doctor answered in stages, between stops. Of course he had ideas about how some of the problems might be lessened, and he would welcome the chance to try them, but he tended not to dream big, not from day to day. He didn't let himself. The root causes of homelessness were old and various, and included, on the national level, a skewed economy and an indifferent government—a constellation of causes that lay far from a cure. "But," the doctor said, "the clean socks we can do."

———————

Not long before midnight, the van stopped beside a little park, Curley Park, half a block from Faneuil Hall and near Quincy Market. It was a tourist spot by day. At night it was occupied by several of the doctor's patients.

The park's benches were arranged in a semicircle around a lifelike bronze statue of James Michael Curley—congressman, governor, and four-term Boston mayor, a child of Irish immigrants who had remained immensely popular among the city's working class, even while serving part of his fourth mayoral term in prison for bribery. Paul's grandparents had probably voted for him. Yet another statue of Curley was seated on one of the benches. The light was dim there, but there was enough of it to see the bronze mayor frozen in a pose clearly meant to suggest that he was talking to whoever was sitting at the bench's other end. Just now, that person was a man called Bobby No Shoes, who was conducting a spirited but incoherent argument with the statue when the doctor approached, Paul following.

A lanky-looking figure was sitting on one of the other benches—alone and with his head bowed over his knees. When the doctor introduced Paul, the man looked up, and in the dim light Paul could make out the gaps where the man's front teeth should have been. Paul thought the guy looked scared. His clothes looked clean, though, and when he spoke, it was clear that he was sober. He said his name was Tim.

Tim. It gave Paul a start to hear his brother's name assigned to a man living on a bench.

Paul sat down beside him and asked how he was doing tonight, and Tim said he was okay but tired. Starting a little before dawn and for about three hours a day, he delivered newspapers downtown. But he didn't make much, not nearly enough to have a place of his own.

Did he know the other people in the park tonight? Paul asked.

Yes, they were drunks, Tim said. And there were some others here tonight he didn't know. He didn't like it when there were strangers around. He didn't feel safe with them around.

It must be hard to live out here, Paul said, and Tim replied that he'd been given an apartment for a while, but he'd had to share it with a roommate. "That didn't work," Tim said. He added, by way of explaining why he was living in the park, "I'm not a shelter guy." And then, after a little more quiet talk, Tim said he was "bipolar."

"I'm bipolar, too," said Paul. "Whatever bipolar means."

Over on Mayor Curley's bench, a very drunk woman had joined Bobby No Shoes. They were sitting with their arms draped over each other's shoulders, laughing raucously about something, their voices mingling with music from across North Street. There was a row of bars and restaurants over there, with lighted signs of varied colors in their windows and over their windows, a festive array, which made you think of lighted Christmas trees standing in the dark. The night obscured a great deal. In the half-light of the little park, the hard times recorded on Tim's face were mostly hidden.

Paul was having long thoughts: What flavor of bipolar afflicted this guy Tim? Maybe Tim's variety had caused him to do something bizarre periodically, something that had got him fired over and over again. A person could do some odd things when hypomanic, Paul knew, and they were things that would get you fired from a lot of jobs more quickly than from software engineering. Sitting on the bench beside Tim, Paul thought about a remark that a few friends of his had made over the last two years. When Paul had told them how uncomfortable he felt about his Kayak fortune, several had replied, "You shouldn't feel that way. You worked hard for your money." The implication Paul heard was that poor people wouldn't be poor if they weren't lazy. *But I didn't actually work that hard,* Paul thought. *I'm just good at something that makes a lot of money.*

———

In retrospect, Paul felt that the van ride had given him a picture of a problem for which there were no apps, no solution that was scalable. But wasn't there value in repeated acts of succor and kindness that didn't in themselves amount to social progress? For him, the night had turned when Dr. O'Connell had said, "But the clean socks we can do." Paul remembered thinking: *If you change a homeless person's socks, that's something. Okay, I know how to alleviate some suffering.*

There was an immediacy to everything about Paul, an apparent need to keep moving, not only an urge to get things done but also a directness and simplicity of feeling. At least to some degree, these were traits he shared with Tom White, the man who, on encountering a starving child in Haiti, had said, "Put in a feeding program here! I'll pay for it."

Tom's example—dying with almost no money of his own after a lifetime of passionate giving—had long since become for Paul something like a father's expectations. Paul had neglected them over the past year, while dreaming up Blade in the midst of intermittent hypomania. Now he was making up for lost time.

Tom had supported causes for the poor in Boston, and more than ever Paul felt drawn to do the same, to help unlucky people in the place where he came from. He planned to spend a third of his philanthropy in Boston—both the $40 million he'd set aside in trust and whatever else he might make in years to come—and some of it would go to Jim O'Connell's programs for the homeless.

But to follow Tom, one had to work in Haiti. Paul flew there a few weeks after his night among the homeless. A year and eight trips after that, he had founded an organization called Summits Education, a collaboration with the Haitian branch of Partners In Health and the Haitian Ministry of Education. It was an attempt to address the dismal state of schooling in Haiti, where most children learned by rote facts that were all too often incorrect; where many schools lacked even one bathroom, an absence that prevented girls from regularly attending; where fewer than 1 percent of students got the chance to go to college. Summits had assumed partial responsibility for 356 teachers and 10,000 students in forty-two primary schools situated in the impoverished Central Plateau. The general aim was to make those schools a model of vastly improved, indigenous public education—delivered to Haitians by Haitians, in their native language, Creole. Paul had also bought twenty acres of land for a high school—in his dreams, the equal of Boston Latin.

To manage all of this, Paul had hired an energetic young American, a former mountaineer and teacher who for a time had been obliged to manage Paul's impatience—to remind Paul that this was not an Internet start-up, that he couldn't expect big results fast. By mid-2015, Paul was saying that he hoped to play Tom White to this young man and the project. He would spend ten years and $10 million on Summits, Paul said. Or maybe twenty and twenty of each.

Paul still favored coach seats on most flights, and he still didn't mind returning to Boston on a red-eye or a very early morning flight. Somehow, in spite of his long legs, he could sleep in a cramped airplane seat. He usually awoke a little before landing, to the gray, grim light of the cabin, peanuts scattered on the aisle floor, odors of recycled oxygen in the air, fellow passengers blinking and yawning. Paul rolled his shoulders. When the plane touched down, his legs started jiggling. "Okay. I'm ready to start my day."

2

SOON A NEW POSTING APPEARED ON THE BLADE WEBSITE:

Update December 2015

We are now focusing on a single project.

Visit lolatravel.com for more info

Paul had routinely declared he was *excited* about Blade's fledgling companies. He and Billo and Schwenk worked hard to support them and gave them real money—$250,000 for most, and $2 million for Bevy. And Paul spent a lot of time helping the start-ups build their teams.

In the meantime, though—really, almost before he knew it— he had starting assembling another team, an in-house "Blade team." He hired his favorite student in the entrepreneurship course at MIT, a young Russian physics major who turned out to have a gift for designing user interfaces. He hired a young Brazilian programmer, another favorite from MIT. The kid came to Paul with an idea for a

Blade start-up—an app to make it easy for friends to split restaurant bills. Paul explained to him why the idea was stupid, then added: "But come join me and I'll find something interesting for you to do." Paul also hired a man in his thirties with a distinguished record in marketing and gave him the title Chief of Design for Blade. And also a man in his fifties, an experienced engineer and manager of engineers, a highly regarded CTO. Blade had Billo and didn't need another CTO, but Paul reasoned, "This guy is so strong, I just have to collect him."

He found work for all these people, mainly in helping out the start-ups. But they were skilled professionals and he was paying them market-rate salaries, and most of them weren't really needed for Blade's incubating functions. And yet Paul kept on hiring. Another UI designer, an office manager, a data scientist. What was he up to? In retrospect, he thought he'd been reacting to a growing disquiet with Blade's business plan. "Hiring is my comfort food. When I don't feel good, I hire people."

And then one day he had all of Blade's personnel present themselves to the board. One member was a professor at Harvard Business School. After the presentations, she told Paul that she liked the start-ups but doubted he would ever find a group to nurture that was as skilled and versatile as that in-house team of his. Why not have them create some companies of their own?

It was as if she had described what Paul hadn't known he planned to do. "Let's build something," he said to Billo and Schwenk and the rest of the team. They had plenty of ideas. One of these came from Billo and Paul. They had both looked into using "virtual assistants," people who do office work remotely for a client, over the Internet and telephone. The assistant works from home, usually for several different steady clients. The client employs the same assistant but only when needed, saving the various costs of a full-time employee.

The idea intrigued Billo and Paul, especially its combination of the human and technological. There were a number of online sites offering the services of virtual assistants. Billo and Paul tried out the best-known of these and concluded that they could do better.

So Paul put an intern to work on a prototype app. He liked the early results well enough to call Joel Cutler at General Catalyst. Paul told him they were going to build the best app around for a virtual-assistant business. As Paul remembered, Cutler said, "Good idea. But do it for travel."

Once again Paul felt, with slight chagrin, *Why didn't I think of that?*

Ever since he'd agreed to put $10 million into Blade, Cutler had been lobbying Paul to start and run his own company again. Cutler and another senior partner at GC had dreamed up this idea: Get Paul to build a novel sort of online travel agency, an anti-Kayak that would employ real travel agents.

The idea grew on Paul quickly—as ideas usually had to grow on him if they were going to grow at all. Online travel had been Paul's motherlode, and this would be a very different approach to it. Paul was, after all, the inventor of Gethuman, the online service meant to let the customers of giant corporations deal with people instead of robots. Here was another chance to create a company that modeled great customer service, commercial and public-spirited both, a red phone of a company. He even had a ready-made name for it: Lola. Short for "longitude-latitude." It was a resonant name for Paul, one of the names that he and Steve Hafner had considered for Kayak. Easy to spell, easy to remember, two syllables that rolled off the tongue, as in the old lyric, "Whatever Lola wants, Lola gets."

No robots booking travel this time. Human travel agents would be the essence of the company. "These are *modern* travel agents," Paul said. He imagined them with much the same ardor he had first imagined Blade's office: "We might not even call them travel agents when we launch the company. These are like phenomenal customer service people. Really high energy, they love their job, they're happy, they make you feel good working with them. They type fast, they're very responsive." The plan ran counter to the contemporary trend to turn as many employees as possible into contract laborers. All of Lola, including its agents, would be regular employees with salaries and a full range of benefits, including 401(k) pension plans and stock options.

Most of Lola's agents would work from home, using the latest in travel search technology. Customers would reach them on their smartphones and notebooks through a mobile app—to be downloaded at lolatravel.com—and they would converse via a technology called "augmented chat," or simply by telephone. Maybe the first paying customers would be people with complex travel plans and people who found it tiresome or difficult to book their trips on computers and notepads and smartphones. And, in Paul's vision, those first customers would keep coming back and tell their friends about the company, because they'd find the service it offered so pleasant and efficient. Also comprehensive. Some airlines and other travel companies blocked online agencies from accessing their information. "But you know what technology they can't block?" Paul said. "Humans. And Lola."

The principal investors in Blade were pleased. Indeed, both General Catalyst and Accel were wrangling with Paul to let them buy a larger share of Lola. American Express was also interested in acquiring a piece. Paul named himself and Billo co-founders, the CEO and CTO respectively, and Schwenk vice president of operations. There were delicious prospects: recruitings and hirings; meetings in front of the whiteboard in the Fenway conference room, he and Billo trading ideas, rapid-fire, about the design of Lola's app.

On a chill December afternoon, everything seemed much the same outside the old Blade office. You still approached it as if on one of the tours Paul used to give—down the stairs from Summer Street, along the narrow wooden boardwalk that fronted the wintry waters of Fort Point Channel, and around the corner into what Paul used to call "the sketchy-looking alley." The *funky* green metal door was still there, still the office's main entrance.

It was when you got inside that you began to see the changes. The stage and DJ booth were gone. That once-essential equipment had been packed up and locked away in a storage room out back. In its place were desks, many more desks than before. Only a few months ago, the office had seemed spacious, if anything too sparsely populated for a going concern. Now it seemed almost crowded, full of unfamiliar faces staring at computer screens—a place both busy and quiet, like a slice of Kayak's engineering office, though peopled by a much larger percentage of women.

Thirty-one new people had been hired for Lola in the past few months, Paul's assistant said, and four more just today. And the little teams that Blade had been trying to incubate into companies? They were gone. Two had died, and the other two had their own offices now. The last of the fledglings, Drafted, had left yesterday, she said. And there was more momentous news. They were running out of room for Lola's people. The amigos were looking for a larger space, and when they found it the Blade office would be sublet.

For more than two years Paul had dreamed about all the wondrous things that would happen in this place. The big-bet companies that would flourish here. The soirees and parties that the nightclub would host—some of them had happened. The Blade Truck and the floating Collaboration Fountain, neither of which had materialized, except as phantasms of the fire. One remembered the tours Paul had conducted when the place was a construction site and all its *insanely interactive* features were still phantasms, too. The Blade wristbands, which had in fact directed the fine, expensive sound system to play snatches of the favorite songs of guests as they arrived at parties. The Blade bar's hockey puck, which actually had lit up guests' favorite drinks. The stage and DJ booth that had made the nightclub *rock*.

Paul's assistant looked across the office toward the glass walls of the Fenway conference room, where Paul was just now meeting with his board of directors and Lola's executives. "Paul was unhappy when the DJ booth was removed," his assistant said. He was even more unhappy, she added, about the prospect of subletting this place. But, he had told her, he hoped to make a deal with the tenant so that he could hold a party here from time to time.

In fact, Paul wasn't very unhappy. And he was not embarrassed, or remorseful. He was merely wistful about leaving Blade behind, less the company than the place. The name Blade would be retired, but saved, of course, for future use.

"Fail fast and pivot." In the parlance of the age of high-tech entrepreneurship, this was a meme, a mantra of the New Economy. As a guiding principle, it was vague enough to serve as a license both for acting irresponsibly with other people's money, and also for invention. Of course, failing with one project and turning to another wasn't practicable for most people, financially or psychologically. But even before Paul had the cushion of great success, and before he'd found the solace of Buddhist practice, there had been many times when he'd refused the temptation to cower or give up. The time, for instance, when he programmed his way out of depression with the Xiangqi website, or the time when he maxed out all his credit creating Boston Light and, refusing to feel desperate, managed to drive a hard bargain and sell out for a fortune.

The people who had invested in Paul expected his twists and turns, both his failures and, as the meme would have it, his pivots. Great success was what his investors were after, and great success is hard to prefabricate. In the part of the economy where Paul operated, an investor wanted to place some bets on a person with ability and boldness, with the tendency to turn a job into an obsession and the knack for tossing an obsession away when a better-looking one comes along.

Paul was a creature of the New Economy, but he was also an old American. He was a carrier of a strain in the American character that refuses to be encumbered by the past. It's an ethos that says you don't have to do what your father did, that indeed you don't have to do what you yourself were doing six months ago—or even yesterday. Consistency doesn't matter. Only invention matters.

———————

Brenda was his foundation, his rock, Paul said. Ever since she'd returned for keeps, he had stuck with his antimania drug. After nearly three decades of struggle, the fire was contained. His native enthusiasm, though, was far from exhausted. In an email about Lola, he wrote:

> I was born to make this company. :)
> Rage against the machine.

He and Brenda planned to marry—privately, but Paul imagined a Shake-the-Lake-size party to follow. They still had the house in Arlington, but had moved downtown to an apartment on the waterfront. One early winter evening there, Paul asked her, "Do you mind if I go out and do Uber for a while?"

"Oh no," Brenda said. Her smile was droll. "I have no problem with the fact that you find strangers more interesting than me."

Paul had become a registered Uber driver. He'd done this for re-search. One plan for Lola was to have its customers rate the services of the travel agents, as passengers rate Uber drivers. Paul thought he ought to find out how it felt to be rated by customers.

Uber drivers use their own cars. Paul had enlisted as a driver for Uber X—the less expensive service; its customers expect to get picked up in a clean but relatively inexpensive midsize car, a Toyota Camry, a Honda Accord. Many of Paul's passengers were surprised to find themselves in the latest model all-electric Tesla with its 17-inch interactive screen in the console, and being chatted up by the driver, who was apt to make the most improbable claims.

A high school student from China and her mother and aunt climb in the backseat. The mother and aunt speak no English. After a while Paul asks the girl if she wants to go to college here in Boston. To MIT, perhaps? She says it is her dream. Paul says, "I teach at MIT." Does he really? she asks. "I teach entrepreneurship," he says. "I teach people how to start companies." He adds, "And I'm driving Uber just for fun." Who knew what the girl made of this. *Such an interesting country, America.*

Being a driver *was* fun. "Kind of putting lots of pieces of my life together," Paul said. "Cars. Serving people. Talking with people. Learning new technology." What he liked best was having a stranger in his car, all to himself, for ten to twenty minutes—people who didn't work in technology, people he would never meet otherwise. He was keeping a notebook in which he listed at least one thing each passenger told him. He was doing well as an Uber driver. After forty-nine rides, customers had given him a nearly perfect rating, an aver-age of 4.97 out of a possible 5 stars. Some nights he made as much as fifty dollars.

ACKNOWLEDGMENTS

MY THANKS TO ALL THE PEOPLE WHO LET ME SIT IN ON MEETINGS, or spoke with me directly, or helped me find my way around the several worlds frequented by Paul English:

Jeremy Allaire, Christian Allen, Suzanne Amato, Bill Aulet, Ko Baryiames, Ben Berman, Mike Bernardo, Tim Berners-Lee, Firdaus Bhathena, Dr. Michael Biber, Robert Birge, Young Chun Blom, Ralf Boeck, Larry Bohn, Kate Brigham, Alix Cantave, Ed Cardoza, Craig Carlson, Mike Chambers, Walter Chick, Cassandra Chipps, Marie Flore Chipps, Jack Connors, Scott Cook, Carol Costello, Joel Cutler, Ophelia Dahl, Bob Davis, Drew Devlin, Marie DiCalogero, Esther Doggett, Dennis Doughty, Sam Dunn, Zach Dunn, Gayle Evans, David Fialkow, Ben Fischman, Melissa Fredette, Sameer Ghandi, Giuliano Giacaglia, Jim Giza, Robyn Glaser, Paul Graham, Steve Hafner, Kristen Harkness, Bill Helman, Reid Hoffman, Zach Iscol, Jonathan Jackson, Lincoln Jackson, Steven Ji, Bill Kaiser, Dr. Andres Kanner, Ben Kaplan, Petr Kaplunovich, Kosmas Karadimitriou, Scott Kirsner, Donald Knuth, Rakshit Kumar, Nicholas Lambrou, Bill Law, Bonnie Levin, Tom Madigan, Joe Mahoney, Jennifer Marotta, Amy

Marshall, John Maynard, Todd McCormack, Julie Melbin, Brian Michon, Sidra Michon, Hugh Molotsi, Michael Moritz, Bob Morris, Harry Nelis, Dan Nye, Dr. Jim O'Connell, Rose O'Donnell, Steve Pelletier, Jeff Rago, Bob Rainis, Vinayak Ranade, Steve Revilak, Michael Saunders, Oren Sherman, Gene Shkolnik, Nancy Smith, Raman Tenneti, Adam Valkin, Loune Viaud, Dave Walden, Bill Warner, David Weinberger, Rebecca Weintraub, Michael White, Thomas W. White (architect), Derek Young, Giorgos Zacharia, and Snejina Zacharia.

Special thanks for putting me up in their homes, to Rustin and Randall Levenson, and to Katherine Ellsworth and Pete Petronzio—and also to Alex Attia and Sonia Miranda of the Charles Hotel. Thanks also to my family and for various kinds of assistance to my friends Richard Brown, Stuart Dybek, Ed Etheredge, Miriam Feurele, John Graiff, Jonathan Harr, Pacifique Irankunda, Hanno Muellner, and Kristin Nelson.

I am especially indebted to Karl Berry, Bill O'Donnell, Paul Schwenk, and Brenda White, and also to Paul English's siblings: Ed, Eileen, Tim, Nancy, Dan, and Barbara. I am grateful to Chris Jerome for all her help and counsel, and to Evan Camfield and Derrill Hagood, and I am more grateful than I can say to my editors, Kate Medina and Richard Todd, for what I now realize has been an extraordinary run of generous help and encouragement. Paul English was invariably courteous and forthcoming. I am grateful to him, of course, and also to his hero—and, as he likes to say, chief adviser though deceased—Thomas J. White.

SELECTED BIBLIOGRAPHY

American Psychological Association. *Diagnostic and Statistical Manual of Mental Disorders*. 5th ed. (*DSM-V*). Washington, D.C.: American Psychological Association, 2013.

Angell, Marcia. "The Epidemic of Mental Illness: Why?" *The New York Review of Books*, June 23, 2011.

Ante, Spencer. *Creative Capital: Georges Doriot and the Birth of Venture Capital*. Boston: Harvard Business Press, 2008.

Bentley, Jon. *Programming Pearls*. Reading, Mass.: Addison-Wesley, 1989.

Berners-Lee, Tim, with Mark Fischetti. *Weaving the Web: The Original Design and Ultimate Destiny of the World Wide Web*. New York: Harper Business, 1999.

Black, Chris. "Hub's Growth as BRA Sees It." *The Boston Globe*, October 9, 1980.

Boston Redevelopment Authority. "Diversity and Change in Boston's Neighborhoods: A Comparison of Demographic, Social, and Economic Characteristics of Population and Housing, 1970–1980." Boston: October 1985.

Boyd, D. M., and Ellison, N. B. "Social Network Sites: Definition, History and Scholarship." *Journal of Computer-Mediated Communication* 13, no. 1 (October 2009), pp. 210–30.

Cantillon, Richard. *An Essay on Economic Theory*. Translated by Chantal Saucier. Auburn, Ala.: Ludwig von Mises Institute, 2010.

Cassidy, John. *dot.con: How America Lost Its Mind and Money in the Internet Era*. New York: HarperCollins, 2002.

CB Insights. "The Exceedingly Rare Unicorn VC." November 21, 2013. Accessed online.

Ceruzzi, Paul E. *A History of Modern Computing*. 2nd ed. Cambridge, Mass.: MIT Press, 1998.

Christensen, Clayton M. *The Innovator's Dilemma*. New York: Harper Business, 1997.

CNN Money. "The $1.7 Trillion Dot.com Lesson." November 9, 2000.

Date, K. A., et al. "Considerations for Oral Cholera Vaccine Use During Outbreak After Earthquake in Haiti, 2010–2011." *Emerging Infectious Diseases* 17, no. 11 (November 2011), pp. 2105–12.

Daylight, Edgar G. *The Essential Knuth*. Geel, Belgium: Lonely Scholar, 2013.

———. *Algorithmic Barriers Falling: P=NP?* Geel, Belgium: Lonely Scholar, 2014.

Foran, A., et al. "Specificity of Psychopathology in Temporal Lobe Epilepsy." *Epilepsy & Behavior* 27, no. 1 (April 2013), pp. 193–99.

Gage, Deborah. "The Venture Capital Secret: 3 Out of 4 Start-Ups Fail." *Wall Street Journal*, September 20, 2012.

Ghacibeh, Georges A., and Kenneth M. Heilman. "Creative Innovation with Temporal Lobe Epilepsy and Lobectomy." *Journal of the Neurological Sciences* 324, nos. 1–2 (January 2013), pp. 45–48.

Goodwin, Guy. "Hypomania: What's in a Name?" *British Journal of Psychiatry* 181, no. 2 (August 2002), pp. 94–95.

Graham, Paul. *Hackers and Painters: Big Ideas from the Computer Age*. Cambridge, Mass.: O'Reilly, 2004.

Hafner, Katie, and Matthew Lyon. *Where Wizards Stay Up Late*. New York: Touchstone, 1996.

Healy, David. *Mania: A Short History of Bipolar Disorder*. Baltimore, Md.: Johns Hopkins University Press, 2008.

Hill, C., C. Corbett, and A. St. Rose. "Why So Few? Women in Science, Technology, Engineering and Mathematics." Washington, D.C.: American Association of University Women (AAUW), 2010.

Hofstadter, Douglas R. *Godel, Escher, Bach: An Eternal Golden Braid.* New York: Basic Books, 1979.

Hurd, Duane Hamilton. *History of Middlesex County, Massachusetts: With Biographical Sketches of Many of Its Pioneers and Prominent Men.* Vol. 3. Philadelphia: J. W. Lewis & Co., 1890.

Invstor.com. "How Venture Capital Firms Work." Accessed online.

Isaacson, Walter. *Steve Jobs.* New York: Simon & Schuster, 2011.

———. *The Innovators: How a Group of Hackers, Geniuses, and Geeks Created the Digital Revolution.* New York: Simon & Schuster, 2014.

Juel, V. C., and J. M. Massey. "Myasthenia Gravis." *Orphanet Journal of Rare Diseases* 2:44 (2007), pp. 1–13.

Kernighan, Brian W., and Dennis M. Ritchie. *The C Programming Language.* Englewood Cliffs, N.J.: Prentice-Hall, 1978.

Knuth, Donald E. *3:16 Bible Texts Illuminated.* Middleton, Wisc.: A-R Editions, 1991.

———. *Literate Programming.* Stanford, Calif.: CSLI Publications, 1992.

———. *Things a Computer Scientist Rarely Talks About.* Stanford, Calif.: CSLI Publications, 2001.

———. *The Art of Computer Programming.* Vols. 1–4A. Indianapolis: Addison-Wesley Professional; 1 Edition, 2011.

———. *Selected Papers on Fun & Games.* Stanford, Calif.: CSLI Publications, 2011.

———. *Companion to the Papers of Donald Knuth.* Stanford, Calif.: CSLI Publications, 2011.

Lanier, Jaron. *Who Owns the Future?* New York: Simon & Schuster, 2013.

Lepore, Jill. "The Disruption Machine." *The New Yorker,* June 23, 2014.

Levy, Steven. *Hackers: Heroes of the Computer Revolution.* Cambridge, Mass.: O'Reilly, 2010.

Lewis, Michael. *The New New Thing: A Silicon Valley Story.* New York: W. W. Norton, 2014.

————. *Flash Boys*. New York: W. W. Norton, 2015.

Mao, Z. F., et al. "Course and Prognosis of Myasthenia Gravis: A Systematic Review." *European Journal of Neurology* 17, no. 7 (April 2010), pp. 913–21.

McNeil, Donald G., Jr. "Use of Cholera Vaccine in Haiti Is Now Viewed as Viable." *The New York Times*, December 10, 2010.

Meriggioli, M. N., and D. B. Sanders. "Autoimmune Myasthenia Gravis: Emerging Clinical and Biological Heterogeneity." *Lancet Neurologica* 5 (May 2009), pp. 475–90.

Morozov, Evgeny. *The Net Delusion: The Dark Side of Internet Freedom*. New York: PublicAffairs, 2011.

————. *To Save Everything, Click: The Folly of Technological Solutionism*. New York: PublicAffairs, 2013.

Mula, Marco, et al. "On the Prevalence of Bipolar Disorder in Epilepsy." *Epilepsy & Behavior* 13, no. 4 (November 2008), pp. 658–61.

Raymond, Eric S. *The Cathedral and the Bazaar*. Cambridge, Mass.: O'Reilly, 1999.

Saxenian, AnnaLee. *Regional Advantage: Culture and Competition in Silicon Valley and Route 128*. Cambridge, Mass.: Harvard University Press, 1996.

Stephenson, Neal. "In the Beginning . . . Was the Command Line." Originally published online, and in book form in 1999.

Williams, Sam. *Free as in Freedom: Richard Stallman's Crusade for Free Software*. Sebastopol, Calif.: O'Reilly, 2002.

I reviewed a number of documents that pertained to the sale of Kayak and were filed with the Securities and Exchange Commission. Accessed at www.sec.gov.

For various other facts and figures, I relied partly on the following:

Bank, David. "BroadVision Agrees to Buy Interleaf . . . for $851.6 Million," *The Wall Street Journal*, B12, January 27, 2000.

Business Wire. "Interleaf, Inc. Earnings Reports." April, 11, 1995; January 25, 1996; April 2, 1996; September 30, 1996; May 4, 1998. Accessed online.

Larson, P. "Interleaf: How Did It Double?" *The Motley Fool*, December 2, 1999. Accessed online.

ProQuest. "First Quarter, Second Quarter, Third Quarter, and Fiscal Year Earnings, 2001: Intuit." 2014.

Skift. "The 15 Largest Travel Companies of 2014." Accessed online.

Statista. "Biggest Internet Companies in Selected Countries as of June 2014, Based on Value." Accessed online.

———. "Market Capitalization of the Largest U.S. Internet Companies as of August 2015." Accessed online.

The World Bank. "Market Capitalization of Listed Domestic Companies." 2015. Accessed online.

According to Ming Sun Poon of the Library of Congress, the story called "The Secret Inside the Orange" evolved from the following: "Bajiong Ren." In < Xuan guai lu > / Niu Sengru; Yang Shengjie, commentator and translator. Lanzhou: Gansu Renmin Chubanshe, 1999, pp. 5–7.

My thanks to Mr. Poon for providing the original, and to Carl E. Kubler for translating it into English.

ABOUT THE AUTHOR

TRACY KIDDER graduated from Harvard and studied at the University of Iowa. He has won a Pulitzer Prize, a National Book Award, a Robert F. Kennedy Award, and many other literary prizes. The author of *Strength in What Remains, My Detachment, Mountains Beyond Mountains, Home Town, Old Friends, Among Schoolchildren, House,* and *The Soul of a New Machine,* Kidder lives in Massachusetts and Maine.

tracykidder.com